# UNDER HIS WINGS

## *Meditations*

Frances Blok Popovich

# Under His Wings

## Meditations

### Frances Blok Popovich

"Keep me as the apple of Your eye; hide me under the shadow of Your wings…." (Psalm 17:8, 9a).

"When I remember You on my bed, I meditate on You in the night watches. Because You have been my help, therefore in the shadow of Your wings I will rejoice. My soul follows close behind You, Your right hand upholds me" (Psalm 63:6-8).

Under His Wings: Meditations

by Frances Blok Popovich

2500 Breton Woods Drive, SE

Suite 2051

Grand Rapids, Michigan 49512

Phone 616-455-3809

E-mail: franpopovich@aol.com

Printed by Amazon Kindle Direct Publishing

Cover by RockingBookCovers.com

# Acknowledgments

To my grandson, Brian Popovich, who adapted the entire computer manuscript into digital format.

To the memory of my mother, Anna Vander Waal Blok, who dedicated her life to training her children in the fear of the Lord.

To the staff and residents of Breton Rehab, who have encouraged me, beginning at the time when I fed my husband during the noon hour, and shared the contents of my writings as devotional readings.

Above all, to the Triune God, whose love has surrounded me all my life with benefits.

—The Author

# Profile Page

The author is a retired Wycliffe Bible translator, who has four children and ten grandchildren. With her husband she analyzed an unwritten Brazilian Indian language, and translated the New Testament into the Maxakalí language of Minas Gerais, Brazil.

She has an RN from the Roseland Community Hospital in Chicago, a BA in Career Arts from Dallas Baptist College, an MA in Sociology from the University of Texas at Arlington and a PhD in Intercultural Studies from Fuller Theological Seminary in Pasadena.

The author compiled two bilingual dictionaries: Maxakalí-Portuguese, and Maxakalí-English. She wrote three novels based on her experiences, and two devotional books, one book of meditations, as well as a selection of her experiences, entitled *Forget Not All His Benefits,* published by Reformation Heritage Books.

Dr. Popovich taught missionary candidates in both Brazil and the United States. She retired after forty years of service in Brazil.

## Summary of *Under His Wings*

The book is composed of single-page meditations based on a portion of Scripture. It includes several personal experiences on the mission field and a few memories of caring for an ailing husband who suffered from Parkinson's disease and Lewy Bodies Dementia for 26 years. Andrew Harold Popovich passed away on April 27, 2014.

# Under God's Wings

*Keep me as the apple of Your eye; hide me under the shadow of Your wings, from the wicked who oppose me, from my deadly enemies who surround me* (Psalm 17:8, 9).

David spent many months fleeing from the murderous harassment of his father-in-law, King Saul. His crime? He was more popular with the people than was the king.

In his prayer David pleaded for God to protect him, and used two examples from nature that demonstrate protection and safety. The first is the protection that the eyelid automatically provides for the fragile eyeball from any environmental injury, and the second is the hen that shelters her chicks under her wings from any threat.

Dear friend, when you realize that you are vulnerable, appeal to God as David did. God delights in protecting those who call on Him for safety. God promised: "...Fear not, for I have redeemed you; I have called you by your name: you are Mine. When you pass through the waters, I will be with you, and through the rivers, they shall not overflow you. When you walk through the fire, you shall not be burned, nor shall the flame scorch you. For I am the LORD your God, the Holy One of Israel, your Savior" (Isaiah 43:1b-3a).

Under His wings I am safely abiding,
Though the night deepens and tempests are wild;
Still I can trust Him, I know He will keep me,
He has redeemed me, and I am His child.

Under His wings, what a refuge in sorrow;
How the heart yearningly turns to His rest!
Often when earth has no balm for my healing,
There I find comfort, and there I am blest.

Under His wings, O what precious enjoyment!
There will I hide till life's trials are o'er;
Sheltered, protected, no evil can harm me,
Resting in Jesus, I'm safe evermore.

—William O. Cushing

1

# God Is a Heavenly Father

*Or what man is there among you who, if his son asks for bread, will give him a stone? Or if he asks for a fish, will he give him a serpent? If you then, being evil, know how to give good gifts to your children, how much more will your Father who is in heaven give good things to those who ask Him* (Matthew 7:9-11)!

Jesus taught His disciples in His Sermon on the Mount how illogical it is to fail to trust in God, when we have often put our trust in less-than-reliable human beings without a qualm. If we can trust selfish people to respond to our urgent needs, why can we not trust God to look out for our welfare?

David was a refugee from King Saul's murderous wrath, wandering in the wilderness of Judah. He confessed his trust in God: "I have looked for You in the sanctuary to see Your power and Your glory. Because Your loving kindness is better than life, my lips shall praise You. Thus I will bless You while I live; I will lift up my hands in Your name. … When I remember You on my bed, I meditate on You in the night watches. Because You have been my help, therefore in the shadow of Your wings I will repose" (Psalm 63:1b-4, 6, 7).

The Swedish hymn writer sang of her trust in our heavenly Father:

> More secure is no one ever
> Than the loved ones of the Savior—
> Not yon star on high abiding,
> Nor the bird in home nest hiding.
>
> God His own doth tend and nourish,
> In His holy courts they flourish;
> Like a father kind He spares them,
> In His loving arms He bears them.
>
> What He takes or what He gives us
> Shows the Father's love so precious;
> We may trust His wisdom wholly—
> 'Tis His children's welfare solely.
>
> —Lina Sandell Berg

# God's Love Envelops Us

*Those who trust in the LORD are like Mount Zion, which cannot be moved, but abides forever. As the mountains surround Jerusalem, so the LORD surrounds His people from this time forth and forever* (Psalm 125:1, 2).

These two verses present us with two very graphic word pictures of security. The first is that of Mount Zion, an immovable landmark, which David said was comparable to the security of those who trust in the Lord. The second is that of the mountains surrounding the city of Jerusalem, which he said were a picture of the security God's people enjoy, being protected by the Lord Himself. Just as the mountains were a permanent protective shield for those living in Jerusalem, so the Lord permanently protects His people.

An unknown psalm writer spelled out in detail the extent of God's protective care of His people: "My help comes from the LORD, who made heaven and earth. He will not allow your foot to be moved, He who keeps you will not slumber. Behold, He who keeps Israel shall neither slumber nor sleep. The LORD is your keeper. The LORD is your shade at your right hand. The sun shall not strike you by day, nor the moon by night. The LORD shall preserve you from all evil; He shall preserve your soul. The LORD shall preserve your going out and your coming in from this time forth, and even forevermore" (Psalm 121:2-8).

Safe am I,
In the hollow of His hand.
Sheltered o'er,
With His love forevermore.
No ill can harm me,
No foe alarm me,
For He keeps both day and night.
Safe am I,
In the hollow of His hand.

—Mildred Leightner Dillon

3

# God Rescues His People

*As an eagle stirs up its nest, hovers over its young, spreading out its wings, taking them up, carrying them on its wings, so the* LORD *alone led him* [Israel] *and there was no foreign god with him. He made him ride in the heights of the earth ....* (Deuteronomy 32:11-13a).

This is a word picture of an eagle teaching its young to fly.

In the early stages of the lessons, the eagle flies beneath the tumbling fledgling and restores it to the nest. Here we have a picture of a loving God who rushes to our rescue when we fall.

Dear friend, as Moses reminded the people of Israel, God is a faithful God. The sons of Korah sang: "For this is God, our God forever and ever. He will be our guide even to death" (Psalm 46:14). When we are convicted of waywardness, we must turn to God and confess our sin, asking Him to restore us again.

David testified: "I waited patiently for the LORD, and He inclined to me, and heard my cry. He also brought me up out of a horrible pit, out of the miry clay, and set my feet upon a rock and established my steps" (Psalm 40:1, 2).

I've wandered far away from God—
Now I'm coming home;
The paths of sin too long I've trod—
Lord, I'm coming home.

I've wasted many precious years—
Now I'm coming home;
I now repent with bitter tears—
Lord, I'm coming home.

I've tired of sin and straying, Lord—
Now I'm coming home;
I'll trust Thy love, believe Thy word—
Lord, I'm coming home.

—William J. Kirkpatrick

4

# God Flies to Our Aid

*There is no one like the God of Jeshurun* [Israel], *who rides the heavens to help you, and in His excellency on the clouds. The eternal God is your refuge, and underneath are the everlasting arms...* (Deuteronomy 33:26, 27a).

As Israel approached the borders of the promised land and prepared to claim it in the Name of the Lord, God reassured them that He would not fail to protect and defend them. Moses reminded them that God would surely support them.

In an earlier example God is depicted as sheltering His vulnerable people like a mother hen shelters her chicks: under her wings. Here Moses depicts God as a supporting refuge, whose eternal arms sustain His people. Not only does He support them, He also is pictured as flying—"riding the heavens"—to rescue them.

Is there a more comforting verse for the beleaguered Christian than the one cited above? It reminds us that God is eternal, unchanging, and has pledged to protect His children. He also is reliable, and we are safely supported by His eternal arms.

The Lord Almighty is my light,
He is my Savior ever near;
And since my strength is in His might,
Who can distress me and affright,
What evil shall I fear?

My heart had failed in fear and woe
Unless in God I had believed;
Assured that He would mercy show,
And that my life His grace would know,
Nor was my hope deceived.

Fear not, though succor be delayed,
Still wait for God, and He will hear;
Be strong, nor be thy heart dismayed,
Wait, and the Lord will bring thee aid,
Yes, trust and never fear.

—Psalter 73, Psalm 27

5

# God is Our Shield

*You O LORD are a shield to me, my glory and the One who lifts up my head. I cried to the LORD with my voice, and He heard me from His holy hill. I lay down and slept; I awoke, for the LORD sustained me. I will not be afraid of ten thousands of people who have set themselves against me all around* (Psalm 3:1-6).

This psalm was composed when David had to flee because his son Absalom led a revolt against his father, attempting to seize the throne. The title phrase is often used in the psalms. A shield has only one function that I know of, and that is protection.

Do you feel vulnerable and exposed? David and his supporters had to flee Jerusalem from Absalom and his troops. They took refuge in the wilderness, exposed to the elements. Yet David felt safe enough to "lie down and sleep," because he knew the Lord would shield him from his enemies.

Friend, you can trust the Lord to protect you from whatever threats you are facing. He may not prevent all dangers, but He will be with you as you face them. David sang, "Yea, though I walk through the valley of the shadow of death, I will fear no evil, for You are with me; Your rod and Your staff, they comfort me" (Psalm 23:4).

David, the Sweet Singer of Israel, also sang of his trust in God, his Protector:

> But blessed be the Lord, Who hearkens when I cry;
> The Lord, my strength, my help, my shield,
> On Him will I rely.

> His help makes glad my heart, and songs of praise I sing;
> Jehovah is His people's strength,
> The stronghold of the king.

> Bless Thy inheritance, our Savior be, I pray;
> Supply Thou all Thy people's need,
> And be their constant stay.

Psalter 75, Psalm 28

# God is Our Rock

*I will love You, O LORD, my strength. The LORD is my rock and my deliverer, my God, my strength, in whom I will trust, my shield and the horn of my salvation, my stronghold. I will call upon the LORD, who is worthy to be praised; so shall I be saved from my enemies* (Psalm 18:1-3).

This use to the word *Rock* is figurative, in the sense of being a stronghold and the source of the David's salvation. Paul defines the usage of the word "rock" as being a reference to Christ: "that rock was Christ" (1 Corinthians 10:4). It is used to define an object that is firm and strong, offering support and defense.

David composed this psalm "on the day that the LORD delivered him from the hand of all his enemies and from the hand of Saul" (introduction to Psalm 18). He explained, "In my distress I called upon the LORD, and cried out to my God; He heard my voice from His temple, and my cry came before Him, even to His ears" (Psalm 18:6).

Vernon J. Charlesworth composed the hymn *A Shelter in the Time of Storm*, as a source of comfort to Christians who are passing through a time of severe trials:

> The Lord's our Rock, in Him we hide,
> A shelter in the time of storm;
> Secure whatever ill betide,
> A shelter in the time of storm.

> A shade by day, defense by night,
> A shelter in the time of storm;
> No fears alarm, no foes affright,
> A shelter in the time of storm.

> O Rock divine, O Refuge dear,
> A shelter in the time of storm;
> Be Thou our helper ever near,
> A shelter in the time of storm.

—Vernon J. Charlesworth, adapted by Ira D. Sankey

7

# Why Did God Give Us His Laws?

*When your son asks you in time to come, saying, "What is the meaning of the testimonies, the statutes, and judgments which the* LORD *our God has commanded you?" ...Then you shall say to your son,..."the* LORD *commanded us to observe all these statutes, to fear the* LORD *our God, for our good always, that He might preserve us alive, as it is this day"* (Deuteronomy 6:20, 21a, 24).

The first recorded prohibition in the Bible we find in the second chapter of Genesis, where God told Adam, the first created human being: "Of every tree of the garden you may freely eat; but of the tree of the knowledge of good and evil you shall not eat, for in the day that you eat of it you shall surely die" (Genesis 2:16, 17). God made it very plain that the consequence of eating the forbidden fruit would mean death. Adam and Eve decided that the God was being something of a "kill-joy" to forbid eating this attractive fruit, and decided—urged by the serpent—to risk it, and as a consequence they and all their descendants have or will have to pass through the experience of death.

When Moses led the descendants of Jacob out of Egypt, they camped in the desert of Sinai, where God gave commandments and laws to the people. Here again, He was explicit about the purpose of the law. He said that its function was "for their good always,...that He might preserve them alive".... (Deuteronomy 6:24). But only a few generations later, the Israelites began to ignore God's laws, and to treat them as impediments to their enjoyment instead of as the keys to divine blessing.

Most perfect is the law of God, restoring those that stray;
His testimonies are most sure, proclaiming wisdom's way.

The precepts of the Lord are right; with joy they fill the heart;
The Lord's commandments all are pure, and clearest light impart.

They warn from ways of wickedness displeasing to the Lord,
And in the keeping of His word there is a great reward.

What man can know his evil heart, discerning all his sin?
O cleanse me, Lord, from hidden faults, and make me pure within.

—Psalter 41, Psalm 19

# The Lord Is Our Shelter

*The LORD is my light and my salvation; whom shall I fear?*
*The LORD is the strength of my life, of whom shall I be afraid? ...*
*For in the time of trouble He shall hide me in His pavilion, in the*
*secret place of His tabernacle He shall hide me. He shall set me*
*high upon a rock* (Psalm 27:1, 5).

David praised God for providing him with a shelter while he
was under attack from his enemies. This refuge was the tabernacle,
which was a tent of worship built by Moses. It was located in
Shiloh during the era before Solomon built the temple in
Jerusalem. Even today we can find shelter in worshiping God.

The sons of Korah sang, "My soul longs, yes, even faints for
the courts of the LORD; my heart and my flesh cry out for the
living God. Even the sparrow has found a home, and the swallow a
nest for herself, where she may lay her young—even Your altars,
O LORD of hosts, my King and my God" (Psalm 84:2, 3).

Saints of all ages have found a refuge in God. Augustus
Toplady wrote, "Rock of Ages, cleft for me; let me hide myself in
Thee." Martin Luther wrote: "A mighty Fortress is our God; a
bulwark never failing." Fanny J. Crosby wrote: "He hideth my
soul in the cleft of the rock where rivers of pleasure I see." Edwin
Mote wrote: "On Christ the solid Rock I stand; all other ground is
sinking sand."

Jesus, lover of my soul, let me to Thy bosom fly,
While the nearer waters roll, while the tempest still is high.
Hide me, O my Savior, hide, till the storm of life is past;
Safe into the haven guide, O receive my soul at last.

Other refuge have I none; hangs my helpless soul on Thee.
Leave, ah, leave me not alone; still support and comfort me.
All my trust on Thee is stayed, all my help from Thee I bring;
Cover my defenseless head with the shadow of Thy wing.

Plenteous grace with Thee is found; grace to cover all my sin.
Let the healing streams abound; make and keep me pure within....

—Charles Wesley

# God Answers Prayer

*Come and hear, all you who fear God, and I will declare what He has done for my soul. I cried to Him with my mouth, and He was extolled with my tongue. If I regard iniquity in my heart, the Lord will not hear, but certainly God has heard me. He has attended to the voice of my prayer. Blessed be God, who has not turned away my prayer, nor His mercy from me* (Psalm 66:16-20).

The unnamed psalmist wrote of his joy as God answered his prayer: "Come and see the works of God; He is awesome in His doing toward the sons of men" (Psalm 66:5). David also testified to God's gracious response to his need: "O You who hear prayer, to You all flesh will come. Iniquities prevail against me. As for our transgressions, You will provide atonement for them" (Psalm 65:2-3).

Another psalm-writer testified to God's goodness in answering prayer, and urged his hearers to make a public acknowledgment of God's faithfulness: "Oh, give thanks to the LORD, for He is good! For His mercy endures forever. Let the redeemed of the LORD say so, whom He has redeemed from the hand of the enemy …" (Psalm 107:1, 2).

> Come ye that fear the Lord, and hear
> What He has done for me;
> My cry for help is turned to praise,
> For He has set me free.
> If in my heart I sin regard,
> My prayer He will not hear,
> But truly God has heard my voice,
> My prayer has reached His ear.
>
> O let the Lord, our gracious God,
> Forever blessed be;
> Who has not turned my prayer from Him,
> Nor yet His grace from me.
> O all ye peoples, bless our God,
> Aloud proclaim His praise…
> [He] steadfast makes our ways.

—Psalter 174, Psalm 66

# God Is a Promise-Keeper

*Zion said, "The LORD has forsaken me, and my Lord has forgotten me."*

*Can a woman forget her nursing child, and not have compassion on the son of her womb? Surely they may forget, yet I will not forget you. See, I have inscribed you on the palms of My hands; your walls are continually before me* (Isaiah 49:14-16).

God has lavished His promises on us, which He has guaranteed in His Word. Not only do they guarantee blessings in this life, but they assure us that we will be partakers of the divine nature, and share eternal bliss as co-heirs with Christ in eternal ages.

The apostle Peter wrote to the dispersed Christian Church: "As His divine power has given to us all things that pertain to life and godliness, through the knowledge of Him who called us to glory and virtue, by which have been given to us exceedingly great and precious promises, that through these you may be partakers of the divine nature, having escaped the corruption that is in the world through lust" (2 Peter 1:3, 4).

God's promises are secure, because He never changes (Malachi 3:6). The author of the book to the Hebrews emphasized God's faithfulness: "Jesus Christ is the same yesterday, today, and forever" (Hebrews 13:8).

> Praise, my soul, the King of heaven,
> To His feet thy tribute bring;
> Ransomed, healed, restored, forgiven,
> Evermore His praises sing.
> Alleluia!
> Praise the everlasting King!
>
> Praise Him for His grace and favor
> To our fathers in distress;
> Praise Him, still the same forever,
> Slow to chide and swift to bless....
>
> —Henry Francis Lyte

11

# Reflecting the Lord's Glory

*But we all, with unveiled face, beholding as in a mirror the glory of the Lord, are being transformed into the same image from glory to glory, just as by the Spirit of the Lord....*

*But it is the God who commanded light to shine out of darkness, who has shone in our hearts to give the light of the knowledge of the glory of God in the face of Jesus Christ. But we have this treasure in earthen vessels, that the excellence of the power may be of God and not of us* (2 Corinthians 3:18; 4:6, 7).

Paul's exhortation reminds us of Jesus' words on the Mount: "Let your light so shine before men, that they may see your good works and glorify your Father in heaven" (Matthew 5:16). He explained that our good works should direct observers' attention to our heavenly Father, not to us: "...that you may be sons of your Father in heaven; for He makes His sun rise on the evil and on the good, and sends rain on the just and on the unjust" (Matthew 5:45).

It is probably ordinary human nature to yearn for the approval of the people around us, but Paul wrote that God saved us so "that in the ages to come He might show the exceeding riches of His grace in His kindness toward us in Christ Jesus... For we are His workmanship, created in Christ Jesus for good works" (Ephesians 2:7, 10a). Our "good works" should reveal God's grace and goodness, not ours.

> To God be the glory—great things He has done!
> So loved He the world that He gave us His Son,
> Who yielded His life an atonement for sin,
> And opened the life-gate that all may go in.
> ....
> The vilest offender, who truly believes,
> That moment from Jesus a pardon receives!
> Praise the Lord, let the earth hear His voice!
> Praise Lord, let the people rejoice!
> O come to the Father, through Jesus the Son,
> And give Him the glory, great things He has done!
>
> —Fanny J. Crosby

# Godly Sorrow Produces Repentance

*Now I rejoice ... that your sorrow led to repentance, for you were made sorry in a godly manner, that you might suffer loss from us in nothing. For godly sorrow produces repentance leading to salvation, but the sorrow of the world produces death. For observe this very thing, that you sorrowed in a godly manner. What diligence it produced in you, what clearing of yourselves, what indignation, what fear, what vindication! In all things you proved yourselves to be clear in the matter* (2 Corinthians 7:9-11).

True repentance leads to a significant change in the person who is blessed with this experience. Remorse brings with it grief, but no lasting change in the person's life. Paul described the "repentance that leads to salvation," and rejoiced to know that the Corinthian believers recognized their sins and were eager to humble themselves and confess them in order to vindicate themselves.

The poem below was written by a professing "infidel" who testified to the great change in his life when he turned to the Lord in faith and confessed his unworthiness.

I've tried in vain, a thousand ways,
My fears to quell, my hopes to raise;
But what I need, the Bible says, is ever, only, Jesus.

My soul is night, my heart is steel—
I cannot see, I cannot feel;
For light, for life, I must appeal in simple faith, to Jesus.

He died, He lives, He reigns, He pleads—
There's love in all His words and deeds;
There's all a guilty sinner needs forevermore in Jesus.

Though some should sneer, and some should blame,
I'll go with all my guilt and shame;
I'll go to Him, because His name, above all names, is Jesus.

—James Proctor

13

# Abounding Grace

*God is able to make all grace abound toward you, that you always having all sufficiency in all things, may have an abundance for every good work. ...Now may He who supplies seed to the sower and bread for food, supply and multiply the seed you have sown, and increase the fruits of your righteousness* (2 Corinthians 9:8, 10).

*... where sin abounded, grace abounded much more* (Romans 5:20b).

My dictionary defines "abound" as "to be plentiful or numerous." We who have "numerous" sins may ask God for His "plentiful grace"; or, in the words of the hymn below, for "grace that is greater than all our sin."

God is lavish in His forgiveness. His grace is much greater than all our sin. Jesus explained to His Jewish critics who accused Him of favoring "sinners" with his presence, that His mission was "to seek and to save that which was lost" (Luke 19:10).

Wonderful grace of Jesus, greater than all my sin;
How shall my tongue describe it, where shall its praise begin?
Taking away my burden, setting my spirit free,
For the wonderful grace of Jesus reaches me.

Wonderful grace of Jesus, reaching to all the lost,
By it I have been pardoned, saved to the uttermost.
Chains have been torn asunder, giving me liberty,
For the wonderful grace of Jesus reaches me.

Wonderful grace of Jesus, reaching the most defiled,
By its transforming power making me God's dear child,
Purchasing peace and heaven for all eternity—
And the wonderful grace of Jesus reaches me.

Wonderful the matchless grace of Jesus,
Deeper than the mighty rolling sea; ...
Broader than the scope of my transgressions,
Greater far than all my sin and shame—
O magnify the precious name of Jesus, praise His name!

—Haldor Lillenas

# Palm Sunday Prophecy Fulfilled

*Rejoice greatly, O daughter of Zion! Shout, O daughter of Jerusalem! Behold, your King is coming to you; He is just and having salvation, lowly and riding on a donkey, a colt, the foal of a donkey* (Zechariah 9:9).

*As He was now drawing near the descent of the Mount of Olives, the whole multitude of the disciples began to rejoice and praise God with a loud voice for all the mighty works they had seen, saying: "Blessed is the King who comes in the name of the LORD! Peace in heaven and glory in the highest"* (Luke 19:37, 38)!

Inspired by the mighty works they had seen Jesus perform, the crowd broke into cheers. Having seen incredible wonders worked by this Man, they led the people in praising the One they believed was about to take over the Davidic throne as the long-awaited Messiah.

Among the cheering multitude there was only One who knew that in fact, He was being escorted into the city where He would be humiliated, whipped, spit upon, and condemned to die on a cruel cross. Jesus had lived all of His thirty-three years in the awareness that He was God's sacrificial Lamb. He knew that within a week He would be led to the slaughter during the Passover festival, fulfilling the ancient prophecies.

As we enter Holy Week and commemorate the final week of Jesus' life on earth, we humbly acknowledge that He took our place and suffered the punishment our sins had merited, so that we might be freely accepted by a Holy God.

Ride on! Ride on in majesty!
Hark! All the tribes hosanna cry;
O Savior meek, pursue Thy road
With palms and scattered garments strewed.

Ride on! Ride on in majesty!
In lowly pomp ride on to die;
O Christ, Thy triumphs now begin
O'er captive death and conquered sin.

—Henry Hart Milman

# Paul's Message

Paul wrote: *We do not preach ourselves, but Christ Jesus the Lord, and ourselves your bondservants for Jesus' sake. For it is the God who commanded light to shine out of darkness, who has shone in our hearts to give the light of the knowledge of the glory of God in the face of Jesus Christ.*

*But we have this treasure in earthen vessels, that the excellence of the power may be of God and not of us* (2 Corinthians 4:5-7).

The Apostle Paul and his associates preached Christ—not themselves—to the Gentiles of Corinth. They were only clay vessels, not in any way remarkable. The glory belonged only to God, Who revealed Himself in Jesus Christ. In His Sermon on the Mount Jesus had emphasized this: "Let your light so shine before men, that they may see your good works and glorify your Father in heaven" (Matthew 5:16i). We must live so that the world can see how good God is, *not* how good *we* are.

> Holy God, we praise Thy name—
> Lord of all, we bow before Thee!
> All on earth Thy scepter claim,
> All in heaven above adore Thee:
> Infinite Thy vast domain, everlasting is Thy reign.

> Hark the loud celestial hymn
> Angel choirs above are raising;
> Cherubim and Seraphim,
> In unceasing chorus praising,
> Fill the heavens with sweet accord—Holy, holy, holy Lord!

> Lo, the apostolic train
> Joins Thy sacred name to hallow,
> Prophets swell the glad refrain,
> And the white-robed martyrs follow;
> And from morn to set of sun,
> Through the Church the song goes on.

> —Te Deum-e- 4th Century
> Attr. to Ignaz Franz, Trans. by Clarence Walworth

# Messiah to the Gentiles

Isaiah wrote: *Behold! My Servant whom I have chosen, My Beloved in whom My soul is well pleased! I will put My Spirit upon Him, and He will declare justice to the Gentiles. He will not quarrel nor cry out, nor will anyone hear His voice in the streets. A bruised reed He will not break, and smoking flax He will not quench, till He sends forth justice to victory, and in His name Gentiles will trust* (Isaiah 12:18-21).

I remember that as a child I envied the Jewish people, because they were God's chosen people. Now I realize that although I am not Jewish at all, God has chosen me for no known reason. Simply because He "so loved the world that He gave His only begotten Son, that whoever believes in Him should not perish but have everlasting life. For God did not send His Son into the world to condemn the world, but that the world through Him might be saved" (John 3:16, 17).

The Apostle John saw a vision of in which redeemed people "out of every tribe and tongue and people and nation" were "made kings and priests to God" and would "reign on the earth" (Revelation 5:9, 10).

Isaiah wrote: "Now it shall come to pass in the latter days that the mountain of the LORD's house shall be established on the top of the mountains, ... and all nations shall flow to it" (Isaiah 2:2).

Abundant fields of grain shall wave
All white for harvesting,
And boundless joy and gladness fill the city of the King.

His Name, enduring like the sun,
Shall ever be confessed;
All nations shall be blest in Him, all men shall call Him blest.

Blest be His great and glorious Name
Forevermore, Amen,
And let His glory fill the earth from shore to shore, Amen.

—Psalter 195, Psalm 72

17

# Faith Is More Precious Than Gold

*...The genuineness of your faith, being much more precious than gold that perishes, though it is tested by fire, may be found to praise, honor, and glory at the revelation of Jesus Christ, whom having not seen you love. Though now you do not see Him, yet believing, you rejoice with joy inexpressible and full of glory, receiving the end of your faith—the salvation of your souls* (1 Peter 1:7-9).

The apostle Peter wrote to the Jewish Christians who had been scattered throughout the Roman world and were experiencing much persecution for their faith in Jesus Christ. They had never seen Jesus Christ in the flesh, but because they believed on Him with all their hearts, they experienced great joy.

Many of our Christian brothers and sisters throughout the world are also facing persecution because they refuse to deny Christ. Jesus predicted that the last days would see widespread discrimination against God's people. May He grant us the grace to stand firm in our faith, rejoicing in the richness of His love!

The blind poet, Fanny J. Crosby, sang of the "riches of Christ":

> O the unsearchable riches of Christ,
> Wealth that can never be told!
> Riches exhaustless of mercy and grace,
> Precious, more precious than gold!
>
> O the unsearchable riches of Christ,
> Who shall their greatness declare?
> Jewels whose luster our lives may adorn,
> Pearls that the poorest may wear!!
>
> O the unsearchable riches of Christ,
> Who would not gladly endure
> Trials, afflictions, and crosses on earth,
> Riches like this to secure!

—Fanny J. Crosby

# Our Redemption Is Through Jesus' Blood

*...Conduct yourselves throughout the time of your stay here in fear; knowing that you were not redeemed with corruptible things, like silver or gold, from your aimless conduct received by tradition from your fathers, but with the precious blood of Christ, as of a lamb without blemish and without spot* (1 Peter 1:17b-19).

Peter reminded the believers to live bearing in mind that their redemption was priceless, since it had been won by Christ's blood, shed on the cross. He added, "Since you have purified your souls in obeying the truth through the Spirit in sincere love of the brethren, love one another fervently with a pure heart, having been born again, not of corruptible seed but incorruptible, through the word of God which lives and abides forever" (1 Peter 1:22, 23).

Peter affirmed that not only is our redemption priceless, it is also eternal, since God's word is eternally valid. It is the "incorruptible seed" that secures our redemption throughout eternity.

> Nor silver nor gold hath obtained my redemption,
> No riches of earth could have saved my poor soul;
> The blood of the cross is my only foundation,
> The death of my Savior now maketh me whole.
>
> Nor silver nor gold hath obtained my redemption,
> The guilt on my conscience too heavy had grown;
> The blood of the cross is my only foundation,
> The death of my Savior could only atone.
>
> Nor silver nor gold hath obtained my redemption,
> The way into heaven could not thus be bought;
> The blood of the cross is my only foundation,
> The death of my Savior redemption hath wrought.
>
> I am redeemed but not with silver,
> I am bought, but not with gold.
> Bought with a price, the blood of Jesus,
> Precious price of love untold.

—James M. Gray

# A Chosen People

*But you are a chosen generation, a royal priesthood, a holy nation, His own special people, that you may proclaim the praises of Him who called you out of darkness into His marvelous light; who once were not a people but are now the people of God, who had not obtained mercy but now have obtained mercy* (1 Peter 2:9, 10).

Peter appealed to the dispersed Christians that they should live in the world as sojourners and pilgrims so that their Gentile neighbors would glorify God on their behalf (verse 12). To live as pilgrims means to submit to the temporal authorities. "For this is the will of God that by doing good you may put to silence the ignorance of foolish men—as free, yet not using liberty as a cloak for vice, but as bondservants of God" (1 Peter 2:14-17).

Since our consciences are oriented by our culture, we must learn to respect our neighbors' consciences as well as our own. In addition, we must be oriented by God's Word as we try to live for His glory. Our spiritual battle is not with human entities, but with spiritual beings. Our arms are the deeds of love and mercy through which we conquer our foes (1 Peter 2:15).

Lead on, O King Eternal, the day of march has come!
Henceforth in scenes of conflict Thy tents shall be our home;
Through days of preparation Thy grace has made us strong,
And now, O King Eternal, we lift our battle song.

Lead on, O King Eternal, till sin's fierce war shall cease
And holiness shall whisper the sweet Amen of peace;
For not with swords loud clashing, nor roll of stirring drums—
With deeds of love and mercy the heavenly kingdom comes.

Lead on, O King Eternal, we follow not with fears!
For gladness breaks like morning where're Thy face appears;
Thy cross is lifted o'er us, we journey in its light;
The crown awaits the conquest; lead on, O God of might.

—Ernest W. Shurtleff

# Christian Fellowship

*Finally, all of you be of one mind, having compassion for one another, love as brothers, be tenderhearted, be courteous, not returning evil for evil or reviling for reviling, but on the contrary blessing, knowing that you were called to this, that you may inherit a blessing* (1 Peter 3:8, 9).

Peter reminded the dispersed Christians to live in accord with each other, to be kind and courteous, even when not treated courteously. He emphasized this by pointing out that they were called to be a blessing to others, regardless of the treatment they received themselves.

He quoted from Psalms 34, 37:

"He who would love life and see good days, let him refrain his tongue from evil and his lips from speaking deceit. Let him turn away from evil and do good; let him seek peace and pursue it. For the eyes of the Lord are on the righteous and His ears are open to their prayers, but the face of the Lord is against those who do evil" (1 Peter 3:10-12).

Out in the highways and byways of life,
Many are weary and sad;
Carry the sunshine where darkness is rife,
Making the sorrowing glad.

Tell the sweet story of Christ and His love,
Tell of His power to forgive;
Others will trust Him, if only you prove
True, every moment you live.

Give as 'twas given to you in your need,
Love as the Master loved you;
Be to the helpless a helper indeed,
Unto your mission be true.

Make me a blessing, make me a blessing,
Out of my life may Jesus shine....

—Ira B. Wilson

# Suffering for Doing Good

*When you do good and suffer, if you take it patiently, this is commendable before God. For to this you were called, because Christ also suffered for us, leaving us an example, that you should follow His steps* (1 Peter 2:20b, 21).

Peter went on to describe Christ's exemplary conduct under persecution: "Who committed no sin, nor was deceit in His mouth; who, when He was reviled, did not revile in return, when He suffered, He did not threaten, but committed Himself to Him who judges righteously, who Himself bore our sins in His own body on the tree, that we, having died to sins, might live for righteousness—by whose stripes you were healed. For you were like sheep going astray, but have now returned to the Shepherd and Overseer of your souls" (1 Peter 2:22-25).

Dear friend, Christ left us an example of how we are to conduct ourselves when falsely accused. How ready we are to complain when we are wronged!

O to be like Thee! Blessed Redeemer,
This is my constant longing and prayer;
Gladly I'll forfeit all of earth's treasures,
Jesus, Thy perfect likeness to wear.

O to be like Thee, full of compassion,
Loving, forgiving, tender and kind;
Helping the helpless, cheering the fainting,
Seeking the wandering sinner to find.

O to be like Thee! Lowly in spirit,
Holy and harmless, patient and brave;
Meekly enduring cruel reproaches,
Willing to suffer others to save.

O to be like Thee, O to be like Thee,
Blessed Redeemer, pure as Thou art;
Come in Thy sweetness, come in Thy fullness;
Stamp Thine own image deep on my heart.

—Thomas O. Chisholm

# Reminders

*But the end of all things is at hand; therefore be serious and watchful in your prayers. And above all things have fervent love for one another, for love will cover a multitude of sins. Be hospitable to one another without grumbling. As each one has received a gift, minister it to one another, as good stewards of the manifold grace of God* (1 Peter 4:7-10).

The aging apostle reminded the dispersed Christians that love for the brethren is of primary importance. In a world where we are surrounded by those hostile to the gospel, we must remember to give priority to demonstrating God's love to the world, especially to those who Jesus loves so much that He died for them. This love may help them to face the tribulation with courage, reassured of God's undying love for them. He stressed the homely virtue of hospitality as essential to this demonstration of love.

Peter goes on to remind them to use the spiritual gifts they have received to serve their brothers and sisters in the faith (1 Corinthians 14). This would be good stewardship of God's gift of grace.

Dear friend, only a service rendered in love can truly communicate God's love to a brother or sister.

O Master, let me walk with Thee
In lowly paths of service free;
Tell me Thy secret, help me bear
The strain of toil, the fret of care.

Help me the slow of heart to move
By some clear winning word of love;
Teach me the wayward feet to stay,
And guide them in the homeward way.

Teach me Thy patience, still with Thee
In sweeter, dearer company;
In work that keeps faith sweet and strong,
In trust that triumphs over wrong.

—Washington Gladden

# Bring Your Worries to God

*Therefore humble yourselves under the mighty hand of God, that He may exalt you in due time, casting all your care upon Him, for He cares for you* (1 Peter 5:6, 7).

Peter reminded the elder believers to "shepherd the flock," and the younger believers to submit to the elders among them, as they submit to God's sovereignty.

He further urged them to bring all their worries to God, because He cared about them. In this He reminds us of Jesus' words to His disciples: "If God so clothes the grass of the field, which today is, and tomorrow is thrown into the oven, will He not much more clothe you, O you of little faith? Therefore do not worry, saying 'What shall we eat,' or 'what shall we drink?' Or 'What shall we wear?' For after all these things the Gentiles seek, for your heavenly Father knows that you need all these things" (Matthew 6:30-32).

Peter emphasized that God's children should glorify their heavenly Father by trusting Him to provide for what He knows they need.

> Be not dismayed whatever betide,
> God will take care of you;
> Beneath His wings of love abide,
> God will take care of you.
>
> Through days of toil when heart doth fail,
> God will take care of you;
> When dangers fierce your path assail,
> God will take care of you.
>
> All you may need He will provide,
> God will take care of you;
> Nothing you ask will be denied;
> God will take care of you.
>
> —Civilla G. Martin

# Be On Your Guard...

*Be sober, be vigilant, because your adversary the devil walks about like a roaring lion, seeking whom he may devour. Resist him, steadfast in the faith, knowing that the same sufferings are experienced by your brotherhood in the world. But may the God of all grace, who called us to His eternal glory by Christ Jesus, after you have suffered a while, perfect, establish, strengthen, and settle you. To Him be the glory and the dominion forever and ever. Amen* (1 Peter 5:8-11).

Peter reminds us to be alert to resist our arch-enemy, the devil, who is always searching for a victim among careless Christians. The reformer, Martin Luther, in his day, left us a hymn as a battle cry to remind us that we will surely win the conflict against our arch-foe because Christ has already won the battle for us.

A mighty fortress is our God, a bulwark never failing;
Our helper He amid the flood of mortal ills prevailing.
For still our ancient foe doth seek to work us woe,
His craft and power are great, and armed with cruel hate,
On earth is not his equal.

Did we in our own strength confide,
Our striving would be losing,
Were not the right Man on our side,
The Man of God's own choosing.
Doth ask Who that may be? Christ Jesus, it is He,
Lord Sabaoth His name, from age to age the same,
And He must win the battle.

And though this world, with devils filled,
Should threaten to undue us,
We will not fear, for God hath willed
His truth to triumph through us.
The prince of darkness grim, we tremble not for him—
His rage we can endure, for lo, his doom is sure:
One little word shall fell him.

—Martin Luther

# God's Exceeding Great Promises

*Grace and peace be multiplied to you in the knowledge of God and of Jesus our Lord, as His divine power has given to us all things that pertain to life and godliness, through the knowledge of Him who called us by glory and virtue, by which have been given to us exceeding great and precious promises, that through these you may be partakers of the divine nature, having escaped the corruption that is in the world through lust* (2 Peter 1:2-4)....

What an amazing gift of grace! Peter says that these promises have made us "partakers of the divine nature" by saving us from worldly corruption. Through these promises we may obtain "all things that pertain to life and godliness through the knowledge of Him who called us to His glory and virtue ..."

Through these "precious promises" God guarantees all we need to live the Christian life in a godly manner.

Isaiah reaffirmed God's faithfulness: "Remember these, O Israel.... For you are my servant. I have formed you, you are my servant, O Israel, you will not be forgotten by Me. I have blotted out, like a thick cloud, your transgressions, and like a cloud, your sins. Return to Me, for I have redeemed you" (Isaiah 44:21, 22).

The Spirit breathes upon the Word
And brings the truth to sight;
Precepts and promises afford
A sanctifying light.

A glory gilds the sacred page
Majestic like the sun;
It gives a light to every age—
It gives, but borrows none.

Let everlasting thanks be Thine
For such a bright display;
Which makes a world of darkness shine
With beams of heavenly day.

—William Cowper

# A Precious Promise

*I will instruct you and teach you in the way you should go; I will guide you with My eye. Do not be like the horse or like the mule, which have no understanding, which must be harnessed with bit and bridle, else they will not come near you* (Psalm 32:8, 9).

In this psalm David first celebrates God's forgiveness of his sins, and reminds us of the blessedness of receiving God's pardon. Then after verse six he blesses God for being his "hiding place;" his shelter from life's storms.

In the verses cited above he extols God's promise of guidance throughout the dilemmas of life, but appends the warning that the troubled pilgrim must be teachable in order to receive God's guidance.

Dear friend, the basic needs of the Christian life continue to be to "trust and obey" what God has revealed in His Word.

The sons of Korah sang: "For this is God, our God forever and ever. He will be our guide even to death" (Psalm 48:14). David sang God's promise: "I will instruct you and teach you in the way you should go; I will guide you with My eye" (Psalm 32:8).

Precious promise God has given
To the weary passerby:
On the way from earth to heaven,
"I will guide thee with Mine Eye."

When thy secret hopes have perished
In the grave of years gone by,
Let this promise still be cherished:
"I will guide thee with Mine eye."

When the shades of life are falling
And the hour has come to die,
Hear thy trusty Pilot calling:
"I will guide thee with Mine eye."

—Nathaniel Niles

# Make Your Election Sure

*Therefore, brethren, be more diligent to make your call and election sure, for if you do these things you will never stumble, for so an entrance will be supplied to you abundantly into the everlasting kingdom of our Lord and Savior Jesus Christ* (2 Peter 1:10, 11).

The "things" to which Peter refers are the character qualities he outlined for us in verses 5-7: "add virtue to faith, and knowledge to virtue, self-control to knowledge, perseverance to self-control, godliness to perseverance, brotherly kindness to godliness, and love to brotherly kindness." If we will cultivate the qualities mentioned, he says, we may reassure ourselves of the genuineness of our calling and election. He added: "If these things are yours and abound, you will be neither barren nor unfruitful in the knowledge of our Lord Jesus Christ" (2 Peter 1:8).

Jesus guarantees our "calling and election". He cannot lie and never changes, He said, "All that the Father gives Me will come to Me, and the one who comes to Me I will by no wise cast out. For I have come down from heaven, not to do My own will, but the will of Him who sent Me" (John 6:37-38).

> Lord, I care not for riches, neither silver nor gold—
> I would make sure of heaven, I would enter the fold;
> In the book of Thy kingdom, with its pages so fair,
> Tell me, Jesus, my Savior, is my name written there?

> Lord, my sins they are many, like the sands of the sea,
> But Thy blood, O my Savior, is sufficient for me;
> For Thy promise is written in bright letters that glow,
> "Though your sins be as scarlet, I will make them like snow."

> O that beautiful city, with its mansions of light,
> With its glorified millions in pure garments of white;
> Where no evil thing cometh to despoil what is fair;
> Where the angels are watching—is my name written there?

—Mary A. Kidder

# Assurance

*Nevertheless, we, according to His promise, look for new heavens and a new earth in which righteousness dwells. Therefore, beloved, looking forward to these things, be diligent to be found by Him in peace, without spot and blameless, and consider that the longsuffering of our Lord is salvation....*(2 Peter 3:13-15).

When we wonder why God is so slow to punish the wicked, especially when they are cruelly persecuting His people, Peter says that we need to remember that the same patience that God demonstrated and still demonstrates with us, He is showing with the ungodly, because His patience ("longsuffering") is salvation. "He is not willing that any should perish, but that all should come to repentance" (2 Peter 3:9).

Remember that God permitted the Egyptians to enslave the Hebrews for four hundred years before He freed His people from their tyranny, because "the iniquity of the Amorites was not yet complete" (Genesis 15:16).

When peace like a river attendeth my way,
When sorrows like sea billows roll—
Whatever my lot, Thou hast taught me to say,
"It is well, it is well with my soul."

Though Satan should buffet, though trials should come,
Let this blest assurance control,
That Christ has regarded my helpless estate,
And has shed His own blood for my soul.

My sin—O the bliss of this glorious thought—
My sin, not in part, but the whole,
Is nailed to the cross, and I bear it no more;
Praise the Lord, praise the Lord, O my soul!

And, Lord, haste the day when my faith shall be sight,
And the clouds be rolled back as a scroll;
The trump shall resound and the Lord shall descend,
"Even so"—it is well with my soul.

—Horatio G. Spafford

# Facing the Facts

*If we walk in the light as He is in the light, we have fellowship with one another, and the blood of Jesus Christ His Son cleanses us from all sin. If we say that we have no sin, we deceive ourselves, and the truth is not in us. If we confess our sins, He is faithful and just to forgive us our sins and to cleanse us from all unrighteousness* (1 John 1:7-9).

The figure of "light" represents all that is true, good, and right, while "darkness" represents all that is false and evil. If we try to convince ourselves that we are living according to God's rules, while doing our own thing and denying facts, we do no more than deceive ourselves, trying to convince ourselves that we've done nothing wrong. But if we confess that we are seriously "off track" as far as righteousness is concerned, God has pledged to forgive us our sins and to render us faultless in Christ's righteousness.

We have God's verdict that we are guilty (Psalm 14:2, 3; Isaiah 53:6; Romans 3:23), and until we confess that His verdict is true, there is no cleansing from our sins.

Blessed be the Fountain of blood
To a world of sinners revealed;
Blessed be the dear Son of God—
Only by His stripes we are healed.
Though I've wandered far from His fold,
Bringing to my heart pain and woe—
Wash me in the blood of the Lamb,
And I shall be whiter than snow.

Father, I have wandered from Thee,
Often has my heart gone astray,
Crimson do my sins seem to me—
Water cannot wash them away.
Jesus, to that Fountain of Thine,
Leaning on Thy promise I go.
Cleanse me by that washing divine,
And I shall be whiter than snow.

—Eden R. Latta

# Jesus, Our Advocate

*My little children, these things I write to you, so that you may not sin. And if anyone sins, we have an Advocate with the Father, Jesus Christ the righteous. And He Himself is the propitiation for our sins, and not for ours only but also for the whole world* (1 John 2:1, 2).

The writer of the Book to the Hebrews reassured the believers that "…. because He [Christ] continues forever, [He] has an unchangeable priesthood. He is also able to save to the uttermost those who come to God through Him, since He always lives to make intercession for them" (Hebrews 7:24, 25).

In His high priestly prayer Jesus left us a pattern of His role as our eternal High Priest: "I do not pray that You should take them out of the world, but that You should keep them from the evil one. They are not of the world, just as I am not of the world. Sanctify them by Your truth. Your word is truth. As You sent Me into the world, I also have sent them into the world…. I do not pray for these alone, but also for those who will believe in Me through their word" (John 17:15-18, 20).

Even after completing His mediatorial work, our Savior continues to be involved on our behalf in His intercessory role. Dear friend, He ever prays for us!

Arise, my soul, arise; shake off thy guilty fears;
The bleeding Sacrifice in my behalf appears;
Before the throne my Surety stands,
My name is written on His hands.

He ever lives above, for me to intercede;
His all-redeeming love, His precious blood to plead.
His blood atoned for all our race,
And sprinkles now the Throne of Grace.

Five bleeding wounds He bears, received on Calvary,
They pour effectual prayers, they strongly plead for me:
"Forgive him, O forgive," they cry,
"Nor let that ransomed sinner die."

—Charles Wesley

# Our Divine Representative

*My little children, these things I write you, so that you may not sin. And if anyone sins, we have an advocate with the Father, Jesus Christ, the righteous. And He Himself is the propitiation for our sins, and not for ours only but also for the whole world* (1 John 2:1, 2).

My World Book Dictionary (1976 Edition) defines an advocate as "one who pleads or argues publicly for something, such as a proposal, belief, or theory; a supporter." Here the apostle John encourages the persecuted believers that even when they sin, they can count on the Savior to support them before God the Father. He explains that since Christ atoned for the sin, His merits are sufficient to justify the guilty sinner.

The author of the book to the Hebrews explained that Jesus "is also able to save to the uttermost those who come to God through Him, since He always lives to make intercession for them" (Hebrews 7:25).

Not only did our Savior come into our world to become one of us; not only did He take on the sin of the whole world when He suffered and died on the cross, but He continues to act on our behalf before the Father. Hallelujah; what a Savior!

> I lay my sins on Jesus, the spotless Lamb of God,
> He bears them all, and frees us from the accursed load.
> I bring my guilt to Jesus, to wash my crimson stains
> White in His blood most precious, till not a spot remains.
>
> I lay my wants on Jesus—all fullness dwells in Him;
> He heals all my diseases, He doth my soul redeem.
> I lay my griefs on Jesus, my burdens and my cares,
> He from them all releases, He all my sorrows shares.
>
> I long to be like Jesus, loving, lowly, mild;
> I long to be like Jesus—the Father's holy Child.
> I long to be with Jesus, amid the heavenly throng,
> To sing with saints His praises, to learn the angels' song.

—Horatius Bonar

# Children of God

*Behold, what manner of love the Father has bestowed on us, that we should be called children of God! Therefore the world does not know us, because it did not know Him. Beloved, now we are children of God, and it has not yet been revealed what we shall be, but we know that when He is revealed, we shall be like Him, for we shall see Him as He is. And everyone who has this hope in Him purifies himself just as He is pure* (1 John 3:1-3).

The aged apostle John still marveled at God's incredible mercy while he was imprisoned on the Isle of Patmos for the sake of the gospel. Not only did God send His only Son into the world to bear our sins and merit salvation for us, but He adopts us as His children! And since the world cruelly rejected the Lord's Messiah, we cannot marvel that it also rejects us, who have been included in the Family of God.

Not only does God accept the repentant sinner as His child, He also has promised us that we will one day be moral images of our Savior—"we shall be like Him, for we shall see Him as He is!"

Sweet bonds that unite all the children of peace,
And thrice-blessed Jesus, whose love cannot cease.
Though oft from Thy presence in sadness I roam,
I long to behold Thee in glory at home!

Whate'er Thou deniest, O give me Thy grace,
The Spirit's sure witness, and smiles of Thy face;
Inspire me with patience to wait at Thy throne
And find even now a sweet foretaste of home.

I long, dearest Lord in Thy beauty to shine,
No more as an exile in sorrow to pine.
And in Thy dear image to rise from the tomb,
With glorified millions, to praise Thee at home.

Home, home, sweet, sweet home!
Prepare me, dear Savior, for heaven my home.

—David Denham

# Acknowledging the Son

*Whoever denies the Son does not have the Father either. He who acknowledges the Son has the Father also* (1 John 2:23).

*...Anyone who has rejected Moses' law dies without mercy on the testimony of two or three witnesses. Of how much more punishment, do you suppose, will he be thought worthy who has trampled the Son of God underfoot, counted the blood of the covenant by which he was sanctified a common thing, and insulted the Spirit of grace* (Hebrews 10:26-29)?

The Apostle John (see the first verse above), was with his colleague Simon Peter shortly after the Pentecost event when three thousand Jews and proselytes had been converted following Peter's Pentecost sermon in Acts 2. They were headed for a prayer service when accosted by a lame man who asked them for alms. Peter courteously replied that he had no money, but was happy to share what he did have, and that was the good news that Jesus of Nazareth heals (verse 6). He took the man by the hand and raised him up on his feet, miraculously able to support the lame man's weight for the first time. Peter then preached a powerful message.

The act created a great stir in the temple, and the religious leaders promptly arrested the apostles for preaching and healing in Jesus' name. Taken before the Sanhedrin, the apostles defended the healing act as giving priority to God's will (Acts 4:19, 20). God sent His Son and endorsed His ministry (John 3:22).

Jesus! The name that charms our fears,
That bids our sorrows cease;
'Tis music in the sinner's ear,
'Tis life and health and peace.

Hear Him, ye deaf, His praise ye dumb,
Your loosened tongues employ;
Ye blind, behold your Savior come,
And leap, ye lame, for joy!

—Charles Wesley

34

# Accepted into God's Family

*Behold, what manner of love the Father has bestowed on us, that we should be called children of God! Therefore the world does not know us, because it did not know Him.*

*Beloved, now we are children of God, and it has not yet been revealed what we shall be, but we know that when He is revealed, we shall be like Him, for we shall see Him as He is* (1 John 3:1, 2).

Paul added additional information when he wrote: "The Spirit Himself bears witness with our spirit that we are children of God, and if children, then heirs—heirs of God and joint-heirs with Christ, if indeed we suffer with Him, then we may also be glorified together" (Romans 8:16, 17).

Very little has been made of our future life status as God's heirs in our hymnody, since it is hard to know what God's children will inherit, and exactly what it means to be a co-heir with Christ. It is clear, however, that not only will God restore Adam's original status to redeemed sinners, but His adoption of them and their glorification as His children and heirs will be unprecedented.

What will it be like, to reign with Jesus through all eternity?

Just a few more days to be filled with praise
And to tell the old, old story;
Then, when twilight falls, and my Savior calls,
I shall go to Him in glory.

Just a few more years with their toil and tears
And the journey will be ended;
Then I'll be with Him, where the tide of time
With eternity is blended.

I'll exchange my cross for a starry crown
Where the gates swing outward never.
At His feet I'll lay every burden down
And with Jesus reign forever.

—Charles H. Gabriel

# How We Can Know...

*We know that we have passed from death unto life because we love the brethren. He who does not love his brother abides in death. ...By this we know love, because He laid down His life for us. And we also ought to lay down our lives for the brethren* (1 John 3:14, 16).

*My little children, let us not love in word or in tongue, but in deed and in truth. And by this we know that we are of the truth, and shall assure our hearts before Him. For if our heart condemns us, God is greater than our heart, and knows all things* (1 John 3:18-20).

The aged Apostle John took great care to reassure the persecuted Christians of the early Church. The two paragraphs in the heading above give us four preliminary examples how we can know we are Christians. He specified how we can know that we are God's children by thirteen additional verses in his first epistle (3:14, 15, 19; 3:14, 15, 19; 4:2, 8, 13, 16; 5:2, 13, 15, 19, 20).

When we examine our reactions and motives we can find plenty of evidence to show our fallen natures, and our selfishness. What we long for, is evidence that we have been renewed by the Holy Spirit. The apostle says we can find this evidence if we love sacrificially, as Christ loved, when He gave Himself as a ransom for our sins. But even if we can find little evidence in ourselves, the apostle says that God can see beyond our flaws and failures.

How sweet and heavenly is the sight,
When those that love the Lord
In one another's peace delight,
And thus fulfill His word.

When free from envy, scorn and pride,
Our wishes all above,
Each can his brother's failings hide,
And show a brother's love.

… He is an heir of heaven who finds
His bosom glow with love.

—Joseph Swain

# A Word of Discernment

*You are of God, little children, and have overcome them* [the Anti-Christs], *because He who is in you is greater than he who is in the world. They are of the world, therefore they speak as of the world, and the world hears them. We are of God, He who knows God hears us; he who is not of God does not hear us. By this we know the spirit of truth and the spirit of error* (1 John 4:4-6).

Why are Christians persecuted? Why are they hated for the very fact that they are Christians? The apostle John explains why there is such a low tolerance for Christians: it is because they are aliens to the world system. Those who are estranged from God are also estranged from His people.

In modern times we are urged to be "politically correct," and are encouraged to tolerate all belief systems except Christianity. We Christians are resented in part because we believe in biblical absolutes. This earns us the label of "intolerant".

Unfortunately, we are often unloving to those who differ from us, and even prejudiced against minor differences in interpretation of biblical truths. In other words, we often earn the label of intolerant in our attitude to other professing Christians. We ought to be known by our love for God and for other confessing Christians, whether or not we are in total agreement with them (1 John 4:20, 21).

Lord, speak to me that I may speak
In living echoes of Thy tone;
As Thou hast sought, so let me seek
Thy erring children, lost and lone.

O strengthen me, that while I stand
Firm on the rock and strong in Thee,
I may stretch forth a loving hand
To wrestlers on the troubled sea.

O use me, Lord, use even me,
Just as Thou wilt and when and where,
Until Thy blessed face I see,...

—Frances R. Havergal

37

# How to Test the Spirits

*Beloved, do not believe every spirit, but test the spirits, whether they are of God, because many false spirits have gone out into the world. By this you know the Spirit of God: every spirit that confesses that Jesus Christ has come in the flesh is of God* (1 John 4:1).

John went on to specify that "every spirit that does not confess that Jesus Christ is come in the flesh is not of God. And this is the spirit of the Anti-Christ, which you have heard was coming, and is now already in the world" (1 John 4:2).

In our day, many people believe there is a God, and, of course, that it is a historical fact that Jesus Christ existed. But they do not believe that He is God incarnate, and that salvation is only through Him. John testified of this, when he wrote: "We have seen and testify that the Father has sent His Son as Savior of the world. Whoever confesses that Jesus is the Son of God, God abides in him, and he in God" (1 John 4:14, 15).

Peter's defense to the Sanhedrin made it very clear that faith in Jesus Christ is essential for salvation: "But neither is there salvation in any other, for there is no other name under heaven given among men by which we must be saved" (Acts 4:12).

> There is no name so sweet on earth,
> No name so sweet in heaven;
> A name before His wondrous birth,
> To Christ the Savior given.
>
> And when He hung upon a tree
> They wrote this name above Him,
> That all might see the reason we
> Forevermore must love Him!
>
> O Jesus, by Thy matchless Name,
> Thy grace shall fail us never,
> Today as yesterday the same,
> Thou art the same forever.
>
> —George W. Bethune

# A Basic Truth

*Whoever believes that Jesus is the Christ is born of God, and everyone who loves Him who begot also loves Him who is begotten of Him. By this we know that we love the children of God, when we love God and keep His commandments* (1 John 5:1, 2).

The term "Christ" is not merely a name nor an honorific title. It designates the only divine emissary, the Messiah, who had a preexistence before His incarnation as a human being. He is the unique Son of God, the Savior of the world.

Failure to believe in the "only begotten Son of God" is the greatest sin we can commit, because God announced His unconditional endorsement upon several occasions ("This is My beloved Son in whom I am well pleased" (Matthew 3:17; Luke 9:35; Matthew 17:5). Jesus Himself said, "For the Father judges no one, but has committed all judgment to the Son, that all should honor the Son just as they honor the Father. He who does not honor the Son does not honor the Father who sent Him" (John 5:22, 23).

At the Name of Jesus every knee shall bow,
Every tongue confess Him King of glory now.
'Tis the Father's pleasure we should call Him Lord,
Who from the beginning was the mighty Word.

At His voice creation sprang at once to sight;
All the angel faces, all the hosts of light,
Thrones and dominations, stars upon their way,
All the heavenly orders in their great array.

In your hearts enthrone Him, there let Him subdue
All that is not holy, all that is not true;
Look to Him your Captain, in temptation's hour,
Let His will enfold you in its light and power.

Brothers, this Lord Jesus, shall return again
With the Father's glory, with His angel train….

—Caroline M. Noel

# God Hates Sexual Perversions

*...[God] has reserved* [the fallen angels] *in everlasting chains under darkness for the judgment of the great day; as Sodom and Gomorrah, and the cities around them in a similar manner to these, having given themselves over to sexual immorality and gone after strange flesh, are set forth as an example, suffering the vengeance of eternal fire* (Jude 6b, 7).

In Genesis 19:5 we read about the aggressive type of homosexuality practiced by the Sodomites, from which Lot and the angels were rescued by divine intervention. In 2 Peter 2:10 this perversion is referred to as "the corrupt desire of the sinful nature." Paul wrote: "...God gave them [idolaters] up to vile passions. For even their women exchanged the natural use for what is against nature. Likewise also the men, leaving the natural use of the woman, burned in their lust for one another. Men with men committing what is shameful, and receiving in themselves the penalty of their error which was due" (Romans 1:26-28).

God hates sexual perversions, but we may not say that God hates the perverts. God hates all sin, but He loves sinners, and sent His Son into the world to save sinners, including perverts (Mark 2:17). We read in Hebrews: "...Because He [Jesus] continues forever, He has an unchangeable priesthood. Therefore He is also able to save to the uttermost those who come to God through Him, since He always lives to make intersession for them" (7:25).

O turn ye, O turn ye, for why will ye die?
When God, in great mercy, is coming so nigh?
Now Jesus invites you, the Spirit says Come!
And angels are waiting to welcome you home.

How vain the delusion, that while you delay
Your hearts may grow better, your chains melt away.
Come guilty, come wretched, come just as you are;
All helpless and dying, to Jesus repair.

The contrite in heart He will freely receive,
O why will you not the glad message believe?...

—Josiah Hopkins

# Why Jesus Came

[Jesus said,] *Those who are well have no need of a physician, but those who are sick. I did not come to call the righteous, but sinners to repentance* (Mark 2:17).

After Jesus had called Levi, and commanded him to follow him, Levi (also named Matthew) celebrated by inviting all his colleagues to a feast. Levi and his friends were renegade Jews, who worked for the Roman government as tax collectors. As a class, they enriched themselves by charging more than was due, and pocketing the surplus themselves. The upright Jews refused to associate with them, and were scandalized that Jesus not only searched them out, but feasted with them. We read of another occasion in Luke 19 when He invited Himself to Zaccheus' house, who was one of the chief publicans (tax collectors). Then Jesus defended His action by stating that He "had come to seek and to save that which was lost" (Luke 19:10).

Jesus' mission was to reach out to the outcasts and those marginalized by the larger society. He took time out from His teaching and healing ministry to bless little children and take them in His arms. He touched the untouchable lepers to heal them, He rescued a woman caught in adultery by challenging her accusers (religious leaders) to carry out their sentence if they had no sins themselves (John 8:7). He gave sight to a man born blind, which people believed was the result of someone's sin (John 9:2).

Sinners Jesus will receive; sound this word of grace to all
Who the heavenly pathway leave, all who linger, all who fall.

Come, and He will give you rest;
Trust Him, for His word is plain,
He will take the sinfulest; Christ receiveth sinful men.

Now my heart condemns me not; pure before the law I stand;
He who cleansed me from all spot, satisfied its last demand.

Christ receiveth sinful men, even me, with all my sin.
Purged from every spot and stain, heaven with Him I enter in.

—Erdmann Neumeister, trans. by Emma P. Bevan

41

# Jude's Benediction

*Now to Him who is able to keep you from stumbling, and to present you faultless before the presence of His glory with exceeding joy, to God our Savior, who alone is wise, be glory and majesty, dominion and power, both now and forever, Amen* (Jude 24, 25).

Jude's brief epistle is mostly a warning against the false doctrines that were prevalent in his day. He exposed the insidious infiltrations in very blatant terms, warning the believers to avoid being ensnared by them. He concluded his brief exposé with a reminder that God was able to protect His people from being victimized by the "ungodly men" who had twisted the gospel "into lewdness."

He wrote, "But you, beloved, building yourselves up on your most holy faith, praying in the Holy Spirit, keep yourselves in the love of God, looking for the mercy of our Lord Jesus Christ unto eternal life" ( VS. 20, 21). He concluded this exhortation by telling them how to treat brothers who had fallen victim to these false teachers, and reassured them that God was able to protect His own and to "keep them from stumbling" to "present them faultless before the presence of His glory" (v. 24).

Dear friends, we also need to "build ourselves up on our most holy faith," looking to God, who is able to keep us from straying from the truth. What a comfort it is to know that God is not only able to keep us from straying, but He has promised never to forsake us (Hebrews 13:5).

My soul, be on thy guard, ten thousand foes arise;
The hosts of sin are pressing hard to draw thee from the skies.

O watch and fight and pray, the battle ne'er give o'er;
Renew it boldly every day and help divine implore.

Ne'er think the victory won, nor lay thine armor down;
Thy arduous work will not be done till thou receive thy crown.

—George Heath

# Grace for Repentance

*And I will pour on the house of David and on the inhabitants of Jerusalem the Spirit of grace and supplication, then they will look on Me whom they have pierced. Yes they will mourn for Him as one mourns for his only son, and grieve for Him as one grieves for a first-born* (Zechariah 12:10).

*Behold, He is coming with clouds, and every eye will see Him, even they who pierced Him. And all the tribes of the earth will mourn because of Him. Even so, Amen* (Revelation 1:7).

If we read only the verse from Revelation 1, we might come to the conclusion that the "mourning" mentioned refers to the regret or remorse experienced by those who were responsible for sentencing Jesus to die on the cross, but since the verse is a quote from Zechariah's prophecy, we may conclude that this refers to a genuine repentance, since it is the fruit of God "pouring out the Spirit of grace and supplication" on the Jewish people. And the mourning is described as resembling grief for the death of an only son.

In Revelation's verse we are told that Christ's coming will be visible to everyone, which tells us that it will not be a clandestine event, but a triumphant assumption of His rightful reign.

> Day of Judgment, day of wonders,
> Hark! The trumpet's awful sound,
> Louder than a thousand thunders,
> Shakes the vast creation round!
> How the summons will the sinner's heart confound!

> See the Judge our nature wearing,
> Clothed in majesty divine!
> Ye who long for His appearing,
> You shall say, "This God is mine!"
> Gracious Savior, own me in that day as Thine!

> At His call the dead awaken,
> Rise to life from earth and sea; ...
> Careless sinner, what will then become of thee?

—John Newton

# God's Message to the Churches

[The apostle John wrote:] *I was in the Spirit on the Lord's Day, and I heard behind me a loud voice as of a trumpet, saying: 'I am the Alpha and the Omega, the First and the Last, and what you see, write in a book, and send it to the seven Churches which are in Asia; to Ephesus, to Smyrna, to Pergamos, to Thyatira, to Sardis, to Philadelphia, and to Laodicea'"* (Revelation 1:10, 11).

The seven churches in the province of Asia may typify all the Christian communities of the Church Age. Each group received a unique message from the Lord: words of commendation and words of censure. Of the seven, the Philadelphia and Smyrna groups received only encouragement. Laodicea received primarily censure, but the gracious promise that if they repented of their "lukewarmness, wretchedness, misery, blindness, and nakedness," that He would again fellowship with them (Revelation 3:15-22). He said, "As many as I love, I rebuke and chasten. Therefore be zealous and repent" (Revelation 3:19).

If the Lord directed one of these messages to our church today, which would it most resemble of the seven in Revelation? Dear friend, we need to beware of becoming "tepid Christians," because God finds them nauseous. He said, "So then, because you are lukewarm and neither cold nor hot, I will vomit you out of my mouth" (Revelation 3:16)!

Father, hear Thy children's call, humbly at Thy feet we fall,
Prodigals, confessing all: we beseech Thee, hear us.

Christ, beneath Thy cross we blame all our life of sin and shame;
Penitent, we breathe Thy Name: we beseech Thee, hear us.

Holy Spirit, grieved and tried, oft forgotten and denied,
Now we mourn our stubborn pride: we beseech Thee, hear us.

We Thy call have disobeyed, into paths of sin have strayed,
And repentance have delayed: we beseech Thee, hear us.

Sick, we come to Thee for cure, guilty, seek Thy mercy sure,
Evil, long to be made pure: we beseech Thee, hear us.

—Thomas B. Pollock

# Heaven's New Song

*And they* [the four living creatures and the twenty-four elders] *sang a new song, saying: "You* [Jesus] *are worthy to take the scroll and to open the seals, for You were slain, and have redeemed us to God by Your blood out of every tribe and tongue and people and nation, and have made us kings and priests to our God, and we shall reign on the earth* (Revelation 5:9, 10).

This is an amazing song of triumph that will be sung by the Church Triumphant. What a sight that will be! Can you imagine the unison of all languages, tribes, and people groups? No language or "dialect" will be excluded from this epiphany. The Church Triumphant will be a multitude that no one can number (Revelation 7:9).

When I was a child I remember hearing someone say, "When I get to heaven I expect three surprises. The first will be that some people I expected to see, will not be there. The second will be that that some people I never expected to see, *will* be there. But the greatest marvel will be that I got there at all."

Jesus prayed for those who believe on Him: "Father, I desire that those whom You gave me may be with Me where I am, that they may behold My glory which You have given Me, for You loved Me before the foundation of the world" (John 17:24). He still pleads our cause in heaven (Hebrews 7:25).

By the sea of crystal saints in glory stand,
Myriads in number, drawn from every land.
Robed in white apparel, washed in Jesus' blood,
They now rein forever with the Lamb of God.

Out of tribulation, death and Satan's hand
They have been translated, at the Lord's command.
In their hands they're holding palms of victory;
Hark! The jubilant chorus shouts triumphantly:

"Unto God Almighty, sitting on the throne,
And the Lamb victorious, be the praise alone!"

—John Vanderhoven

45

# The Martyrs' Plea

*I saw under the altar the souls of those who had been slain for the word of God and for the testimony which they held. And they cried with a loud voice, saying, "How long, O Lord, holy and true, until You judge and avenge our blood on those who dwell on the earth?" ...and it was told to them that they should rest a little while longer, until both the number of their fellow servants and their brethren, who would be killed as they were, was completed"* (Revelation 6:9-11).

Though the ages there have been victims of man's rebellion against God, and of Satan's rages against all of God's gracious purposes for His fallen creatures, but there may soon be as many martyrs in this century as there have been in the entire Christian era. In many countries Christians are targeted for abuse and suffering.

Note that God's patience extends to the persecutors. Peter wrote that Christ was delaying judgment on the enemies of the gospel, because "He is not willing that any should perish, but that all should come to repentance" (2 Peter 3:9). He urged his readers, "The end of all things is at hand; therefore be serious and watchful in your prayers, and above all things have fervent love for one another…" (1 Peter 4:7, 8).

Dear friend, let us not forget to pray for our brothers and sisters who are suffering under cruel persecution and want. Jesus urged us to "do to others as we would have them do to us" (Matthew 7:12). If we were undergoing persecution, we would want someone to pray for us.

O for a faith that will not shrink though pressed by many a foe;
That will not tremble on the brink of any earthy woe.

That will not murmur nor complain beneath the chastening rod,
But, in the hour of grief or pain, will lean upon its God!

That bears unmoved the world's dread frown,
Nor heeds its scornful smile;
That seas of trouble cannot drown, nor Satan's arts beguile.

—W. H. Bathurst

# God Comforts the Martyrs

*Then one of the elders answered, saying to me, "Who are these arrayed in white robes, and where did they come from?" And I said to him, "Sir, you know." So he said to me, "These are the ones who came out of the great tribulation, and washed their robes and made them white in the blood of the Lamb... They shall neither hunger anymore nor thirst anymore, the sun shall not strike them, nor any heat, for the Lamb who is in the midst of the throne will shepherd them and lead them to living fountains of waters. And God will wipe away every tear from their eyes"* (Revelation 7:13, 14, 16, 17).

What a glorious picture of the Lord comforting the believers who have suffered persecution and have struggled against the world, the flesh, and the devil, and have overcome!

Some of them died the most cruel deaths the enemies of the gospel could devise, and now they receive their eternal rewards from God. Never again will they weep, or suffer, or die. Never again will they experience hunger, or homelessness, or exposure to the elements. God Himself will be their Shepherd.

Dear friend, God will never abandon you in this life, however lonely you may feel. Paul wrote: "In all these things we are more than conquerors through Him who loved us" (Romans 5:37).

When He shall come resplendent in His glory,
To take His own from out this vale of night,
O may I know the joy at His appearing—
Only at morn to walk with Him in white!

When I shall stand within the court of heaven
Where white-robed pilgrims pass before my sight—
Earth's martyred saints and blood-washed overcomers—
These then are they who walk with Him in white!

When He shall call, from earth's remotest corners,
All who have stood triumphant in His might,
O to be worthy then to stand beside them,
And in that morn to walk with Him in white!

—Almeda J. Pearce

# Blessing on the Overcomers

*Here is the patience of the saints, here are those who keep the commandments of God and the faith of Jesus. Then I heard a voice from heaven saying to me, "Write 'Blessed are the dead who die in the Lord from now on'." "Yes," says the Spirit, "that they may rest from their labors, and their works follow them"* (Revelation 14:13, 14).

It is the faithful sower who is promised a rich harvest. An unknown psalmist wrote: "Those who sow in tears shall reap in joy. He who continually goes forth weeping, bearing seed for sowing, shall doubtless come again with rejoicing, bringing his sheaves with him" (Psalm 126:6). What a wonderful promise, that our works will follow us after we leave this life! Let us then labor for our Master, although the results may not be immediately evident in this life.

There is a land of pure delight where saints immortal reign;
Eternal day excludes the night and pleasures banish pain.
There everlasting spring abides and never withering flowers;
Death like a narrow sea divides that heavenly land from ours.

Sweet fields beyond the swelling flood
Stand dressed in living green,
So to the Jews old Canaan stood
While Jordan rolled between.
But timorous mortals start and shrink
To cross the narrow sea,
And linger shivering on the brink, and fear to launch away.

O could we make our doubts remove
Those gloomy doubts that rise,
And see the Canaan that we love with unbeclouded eyes,
Could we but stand where Moses stood
And view the landscape o'er,
Not Jordan's stream nor death's cold flood
Should fright us from the shore.

—Isaac Watts

# The Bliss of the Overcomers

*You* [Church of Sardis] *have a few names even in Sardis, who have not defiled their garments, and they shall walk with Me in white, for they are worthy. He who overcomes, shall be clothed in white garments, and I will not blot out his name from the Book of Life, but I will confess his name before my Father and before His angels* (Revelation 3:4, 5).

When Christ addressed the Church at Sardis He pointed out that their reputation as a living church was erroneous. In fact, He accused them of being dead. Then He urged them to repent of their lassitude, lest He appear to them while they were not expecting Him.

After this rebuke, He praised the few in that Church who had been faithful to His word, and promised that He would not "blot out their names from the Book of Life."

Dear friend, God warns those who are indifferent believers that He is not satisfied with them. However, He holds out the offer of forgiveness, and promised to reward those who are faithful, and have not "defiled their garments." They will "walk with Him in white, for they are worthy."

> If, on a quiet sea toward heaven we calmly sail,
> With grateful hearts, O God, to Thee,
> We'll own the favoring gale.

> But should the surges rise and rest delay to come,
> Blest be the tempest, kind the storm,
> That drives us nearer home.

> Soon shall our doubts and fears all yield to Thy control,
> Thy tender mercies shall illume
> The midnight of the soul.

> Teach us in every state to make Thy will our own;
> And when the joys of sense depart,
> To live by faith alone.

> —A. M. Toplady

# The Final Judgment

*Then I saw a great white throne and Him who sat on it, from whose face the earth and the heaven fled away. And there was found no place for them.*

*And I saw the dead, small and great, standing before God, and books were opened. And another book was opened, which is the Book of Life. And the dead were judged according to their works, by the things which were written in the books.... And anyone not found written in the Book of Life was cast into the lake of fire* (Revelation 20:11, 12, 15).

After Satan (the "dragon") and the "false prophet" are consigned to the "bottomless pit," God will judge the human survivors, especially those whose names are not written in the Book of Life. They will share the fate of Satan and the False Prophet.

In this final book of the Bible we have many graphic pictures of God's judgment on His rebellious creatures. Even Death and Hades (the abode of the dead) will be condemned to the lake of fire, the bottomless pit. Yet the book ends with an appeal: "The Spirit and the bride say, 'Come!' And let him who thirsts come. Whoever desires, let him take the water of life freely" (Revelation 22:17).

The invitation is followed by a warning: "If anyone adds to these things, God will add to him the plagues that are written in this book, and if anyone takes away from the words of the book of this prophecy, God shall take away his part from the Book of Life, from the holy city..." (Revelation 22:18, 19).

> Sinners, behold that downward road
> Which leads to endless woe;
> What multitudes of thoughtless souls
> The road to ruin go!
>
> Lord, I would now a pilgrim be,
> Guide Thou my steps aright;
> I would not for ten thousand worlds
> Be banished from Thy sight.

—J. Dobell

50

# The Church Triumphant

*There shall be no more curse, but the throne of God and of the Lamb shall be in it, and His servants shall serve Him. They shall see His face, and His name shall be on their foreheads. There shall be no night there. They need no lamp nor light of the sun, for the Lord God gives them light. And they shall reign forever and ever....*

*Blessed are those who do His commandments, that they may have the right to the tree of life, and may enter through the gates into the city* (Revelation 22:3-5, 14).

In the penultimate chapter of this book God promises that there will be no more grief in the celestial city. Also, the victors will never die again, because there will be no more sickness and no more pain. He sums up these blessings by explaining that "the former things are passed away" (Revelation 21:3).

Dear friends, the best is yet to come! Paul wrote, "Eye has not seen, nor ear heard, nor have entered into the heart of man, the things that God has prepared for those that love Him" (1 Corinthians 2:9). An unknown writer urged: "Therefore let us go forth to Him, outside the camp, bearing His reproach. For here we have no continuing city, but we seek the one to come" (Hebrews 13:13, 14).

Ten thousand times ten thousand in sparkling raiment bright,
The armies of the ransomed saints throng up the steeps of light.
'Tis finished, all is finished, their fight with death and sin,
Fling open wide the golden gates and let the victors in.

What rush of alleluias fills all the earth and sky!
What ringing of a thousand harps bespeaks the triumph nigh!
O day for which creation and all its tribes were made;
O joy, for all its former woes a thousand fold repaid! ...

Appear, Desire of nations, Thine exiles long for home;
Show in the heavens Thy promised signs,
Thou Prince and Savior, come.

—Henry Alford

# Creation

*Then God saw everything that He had made, and it was very good. So the evening and the morning were the sixth day.....*

*This is the history of the heavens and the earth when they were created, in the day that the LORD God made the earth and the heavens,...* (Genesis 1:31, 2:4).

The Bible both begins and ends with praises to God as the Creator of the universe. The first book in the Bible chronicles God's creative acts in giving substance and form to our world, while the last book relates that the twenty-four elders bowed down before Him and said: "You are worthy, O Lord, to receive glory and honor and power, for You created all things and by Your will they exist and were created" (Revelation 4:11).

The gospel of John points out that Jesus Christ ("the Word") existed in "the beginning," and was truly God, and that "all things were made through Him, and without Him nothing was made that was made" (John 1:1-3).

Dear friend, the God who created such marvelous beauty and complexity does not change, so He is able and willing to keep His promises (Malachi 3:6). He has promised one day to deliver nature, as well as all humans who have come to Him in faith (Romans 8:19-22).

> This is my Father's world, and to my listening ears
> All nature sings, and round me rings
> The music of the spheres.
> This is my Father's world, I rest me in the thought
> Of rocks and trees, of skies and seas,
> His hand the wonders wrought.
>
> This is my Father's world, O let me ne'er forget
> That though the wrong seems oft so strong,
> God is the Ruler yet.
> This is my Father's world, the battle is not done;
> Jesus who died shall be satisfied,
> And heaven and earth be one.

—Maltbie D. Babcock

# The Origin of the Sabbath

*Thus the heavens and the earth and all the host of them were finished. And on the seventh day God ended His work which He had done, and He rested on the seventh day from all His work which He had done.*

*Then God blessed the Sabbath day and sanctified it, because He rested from all His work which God had created and made* (Genesis 2:1-3).

*Remember the Sabbath day, to keep it holy. Six days you shall labor and do all your work, but the seventh day is the Sabbath of the LORD your God. In it you shall do no work...., for in six days the LORD made the heavens and the earth, the sea, and all that is in them, and rested the seventh day. Therefore the LORD blessed the Sabbath day and hallowed it* (Exodus 20:8-11).

Our Lord Jesus Himself emphasized the importance of the day by reminding His audience that "'The Sabbath was made for man, not man for the Sabbath. Therefore the Son of Man is also the Lord of the Sabbath" (Mark 2:27, 28).

God reminded the people of Judah of the blessings in store for them if they should keep the Sabbath with joy, rather than as an irksome duty, and strive for social justice (Isaiah 58).

O day of rest and gladness, o day of joy and light,
O balm of care and sadness, most beautiful, most bright;
On thee, the high and lowly, bending before the throne,
Sing "Holy, Holy, Holy," to Thee, great "Three in One."

On thee, at the creation, the light first had its birth,
On thee, for our salvation, Christ rose from depths of earth.
On thee, our Lord victorious, the Spirit sent from heaven,
And thus on thee most glorious, a triple light was given.

Today on weary nations the heavenly manna falls;
To holy convocations the silver trumpet calls,
Where gospel light is glowing with pure and radiant beams,
And living water flowing with soul-refreshing streams.

— C. Wordsworth

# What God Forbade

*And the* LORD *God commanded the man, saying, "Of every tree in the garden you may freely eat, but of the tree of the knowledge of good and evil you shall not eat, for in the day that you eat of it you shall surely die* (Genesis 2:16, 17).

It was certainly not hunger that led our first parents to eat the forbidden fruit. They had their pick of all the fruit trees that God had placed in Eden; of all, that is, except one tree. That was the "tree of the knowledge of good and evil."

It seems that Eve was more curious than Adam, because she was the first to pick the attractive fruit, and she urged her husband to try it out. One attraction may have been the title of the tree, which promised to add something unique to their life experiences, but the Bible mentions that the fruit looked appetizing.

Even so, they might have done no more than discuss the tree and wonder why it was prohibited, but then the serpent came and challenged them to check it out for themselves. He also suggested than God probably had some ulterior motive in forbidding them to eat it. The main attraction was probably that God had forbidden them to eat the fruit, and we all know the attraction of a thing which is forbidden! Isaiah wrote: "All we like sheep have gone astray; we have turned everyone to his own way… (Isaiah 53:6).

> Awake, my soul, to joyful lays
> And sing my great Redeemer's praise;
> He justly claims a song from me:
> His loving kindness, O how free!
>
> He saw me ruined by the fall,
> Yet loved me, notwithstanding all;
> He saved me from my lost estate:
> His loving kindness, O how great!
>
> Often I feel my sinful heart,
> Prone from my Savior to depart;
> But though I oft have Him forgot,
> His loving kindness changes not.
>
> —Samuel Medley

# Passing the Buck

[God asked], *"Who told you that you were naked? Have you eaten from the tree of which I commanded you that you should not eat?"*

*Then the man said, "The women whom You gave to be with me, she gave me of the tree, and I ate."*

*And the LORD God said to the woman, "What is this you have done?" The woman said, "The serpent deceived me, and I ate"* (Genesis 3:11-13).

In their first act as sinners, our first parents tried to excuse themselves by blaming someone else. What they said was true, but they forgot to mention that they willingly committed this transgression against God's law. The serpent tempted them; it did not force them to eat the forbidden fruit.

The apostle Paul wrote: "And Adam was not deceived, but the woman being deceived fell into transgression" (1 Timothy 2:14). So it seems that Adam sinned because he tried to please his wife, not because the serpent had convinced him, as it had Eve.

Ever since then it seems to have become a habit to throw the blame for our sins on someone else. But God wants us to face up to our sins and confess them.

> In Thy wrath and hot displeasure,
> Chasten not Thy servant, Lord,
> Let Thy mercy, without measure,
> Help and peace to me afford.

> Heavy is my tribulation,
> Sore my punishment has been;
> Broken by Thy indignation,
> I am troubled by my sin.

> With my burden of transgression,
> Heavy laden, overborne,
> Humbled low I make confession,
> For my folly now I mourn.

—Psalter 102, Psalm 38

# The First Promise of Redemption

*So the LORD God said to the serpent: "Because you have done this, you are cursed more than the cattle, and more than every beast of the field. On your belly you shall go, and you shall eat dust every day of your life. And I will put enmity between you and the woman, and between your seed and her seed. He shall bruise your head, and you shall bruise His heel"* (Genesis 3:14, 15).

When God initiated His interrogation He began with Adam and ended with the serpent, but in pronouncing His sentences, He began with the serpent and ended with Adam.

The Serpent—also known as Satan or the Devil—is God's enemy. He is believed to be a rebel angel who God expelled from heaven with his cohorts. He set about to ruin God's perfect creation. God pronounced his doom (his head would be "bruised"), while the woman's descendant's heel would be "bruised." God said there is lasting enmity between the evil spirits and human beings.

As soon as the first couple sinned, God promised they would be redeemed by one of their descendants. Later God promised Abraham that all the nations of the earth would be blessed though his descendants (Genesis 12:3; 18:18).

The apostle Peter warned the early Christians to be alert and to resist the Devil: "Be sober, be vigilant, because your adversary the devil walks about like a roaring lion, seeking whom he may devour. Resist him, steadfast in the faith, knowing that the same sufferings are experienced by your brothers in the world" (1 Peter 5:8, 9).

And though this world with devils filled
Should threaten to undo us,
We will not fear, for God has willed
His truth to triumph through us....

—Martin Luther

# The First Murder

*In the process of time ... Cain brought an offering of the fruit of the ground to the LORD. Abel also brought of the firstborn of his flock and of their fat. And the LORD respected Abel and his offering, but He did not respect Cain and his offering. And Cain was very angry, and his countenance fell ...*

*Now Cain talked with Abel his brother ...when they were in the field. ... Cain rose up against Abel his brother and killed him* (Genesis 4:3-4, 8, 9).

Murder is a terrible crime, but it is one we have never committed. Or have we?

Jesus said, "You have heard that it was said to those of old, 'You shall not murder, and whoever murders will be in danger of the judgment.' But I say to you that whoever is angry with his brother without a cause shall be in danger of the judgment. And whoever says to his brother, "Raca!" shall be in danger of the council. But whoever says, 'You fool!' shall be in danger of hell fire" (Matthew 5:21, 22).

Have you ever belittled your brother in a moment of exasperation? According to Jesus' explanation, you are guilty and "in danger of hell fire."

None of us has a completely clean slate. No one, that is, except Jesus. The apostle Peter wrote about Jesus: "Who committed no sin, nor was deceit found in His mouth. Who, when He was reviled, did not revile in return. When He suffered, He did not threaten, but committed Himself to Him who judges righteously; who Himself bore our sins in His own body on the tree, that we, having died to sins, might live for righteousness— by whose stripes you were healed" (1 Peter 2:22-24).

Lord, like the publican I stand and lift my heart to Thee:
Thy pardoning grace, O God, command, be merciful to me.

I smite upon my anxious breast, o'erwhelmed with agony!
O save my soul, by sin oppressed; be merciful to me....

—T. Raffles

# The Universal Flood

*Then the LORD saw that the wickedness of man was great in the earth, and that every intent of the thoughts of his heart was only evil continually. And the LORD was sorry that He had made man on the earth, and He was grieved in His heart.*

*So the LORD said, "I will destroy man whom I have created from the face of the earth, both man and beast, creeping thing and birds of the air, for I am sorry that I made them." But Noah found grace in the eyes of the LORD* (Genesis 6:5-8).

What had been a delight to God's heart was now ruined by Satan's manipulation and man's tendency to evil. God determined to destroy most of what He had created; yet He tempered this judgment because of the righteousness of one man: Noah. When God warned him of the judgment that was pending, Noah obediently built an ark so that his family and a sampling of animals might be saved. Thus "he became an heir of the righteousness which is according to faith" (Hebrews 11:7).

The flood lasted 150 days, but it took longer before the earth had sufficiently dried to enable them to leave the ark. Then God promised: "I will never again curse the ground for man's sake, although the imagination of man's heart is evil from his youth. Nor will I again destroy every living thing as I have done. While the earth remains, seedtime and harvest, cold and heat, winter and summer, and day and night shall not cease" (Genesis 8:21, 22). And God put a rainbow in the clouds as a memorial.

Let hearts rejoice that seek the Lord, His holy Name adore;
Seek ye Jehovah and His strength,
Seek Him forevermore.

Ye children of His covenant, who of His grace have heard,
Forget not all His wondrous deeds
And judgments of His word.

The Lord our God is God alone, all lands His judgments know;
His promise He remembers still, while generations go.

—Psalter 289, Psalm 105

# The Monolingual Tower of Babel

*Now the whole earth was one language and one speech. And it came to pass, as they journeyed from the east, that they found a plain in the land of Shinar, and they dwelt there. Then they said to one another, "Come, let us make bricks and bake them thoroughly," and they had brick for stone and asphalt for mortar.*

*And they said, "Come, let us build ourselves a city, and a tower whose top is in the heavens. Let us make a name for ourselves, lest we be scattered abroad over the face of the whole earth* (Genesis 11:2-4).

After the flood, God had commanded them to "be fruitful and multiply; Bring forth abundantly in the earth And multiply in it" (Genesis 9:7). Rather than spreading out, as God had commanded, they wanted to consolidate, to hang together. God nipped their plans in the bud by confusing the language of communication, making it impossible to cooperate in the construction project. "So the LORD scattered them abroad from there over the face of all the earth, and they ceased building the city" (Genesis 11:8).

Although the some 3,000 languages in the world still seem to divide us, there is coming a day when the variety of languages will bring glory to God and joy to His redeemed children. John wrote: "and they sang a new song, saying: 'You are worthy to take the scroll and to open the seals, for You were slain and have redeemed us to God by Your blood out of every tribe and tongue and people and nation, and have made us kings and priests to our God, and we shall reign on the earth" (Revelation 5:9, 10).

O for a thousand tongues to sing my great Redeemer's praise,
The glory of my God and King, the triumphs of His grace.

My gracious Master and my God, assist me to proclaim,
To spread through all the earth abroad
The honors of Thy Name.

Hear Him, ye deaf, His praise ye dumb,
Your loosened tongues employ;
Ye blind, behold your Savior come, and leap ye lame for joy.

—Charles Wesley

# Abraham Believed God

*If Abraham was justified by works, he has something to boast about, but not before God. For what does the Scripture say? "Abraham believed God, and it was accounted to him for righteousness"* (Romans 4:2, 3, quoting Genesis 15:6).

In the early chapters of the first book of the Bible (Genesis), we read of several persons who pleased God: Adam (before the Fall), Abel, Enoch, Noah, and now Abraham. The apostle Paul explained that Abraham was justified by faith, in that he believed God's promises and obeyed Him. God had promised the man who was one hundred years old that he would have a son by his wife, who was ninety, although she had never been able to bear children. But Abraham believed God, and God accounted his faith for righteousness.

Are there promises in the scriptures that you have a hard time believing? Abraham also had trouble believing that God would grant him an heir after the many years during which he and his wife had been disappointed. At ninety Sarah had probably gone through menopause and had given up any hope of pregnancy. We know Abraham had other children, but God promised that he would have a son by Sarah. And that was humanly impossible. Yet Abraham believed God.

O for a faith that will not shrink
Though pressed by many a foe,
That will not tremble on the brink of any earthly woe.

That will not murmur nor complain
Beneath the chastening rod,
But in the hour of grief and pain will lean upon its God.

That bears unmoved the world's dread frown,
Nor heeds its scornful smile,
That seas of trouble cannot drown, nor Satan's darts beguile.

A faith that keeps the narrow way
Till life's last hour is fled;
And with a pure and heavenly ray lights up a dying bed.

—W. H. Bathurst

# God Saves Lot from Destruction

[God turned] *the cities of Sodom and Gomorrah into ashes, condemned them to destruction, making them an example to those who afterward would live ungodly; and delivered righteous Lot, who was oppressed by the filthy conduct of the wicked (for that righteous man dwelling among them tormented his righteous soul from day to day by seeing and hearing their lawless deeds)—then the Lord knows how to deliver the godly out of temptations and to reserve the unjust under punishment for the day of judgment* (2 Peter 2:6-9).

In his second epistle, the apostle Peter comforted the Jewish Christians in the diaspora who were undergoing persecution, by reminding them that God had not abandoned them, but that He delivers righteous persons from the clutches of the wicked who would abuse them. He affirmed that "God knows how to deliver the godly" from those who would exploit and persecute them. He saved Lot and his daughters, but they did suffer the loss of all their material possessions.

Fret not thyself nor envious be
When wicked workers thou shalt see
Who prosper in their way;
For like the grass they perish soon,
And, like the herb cut down at noon,
They wither in a day.

Trust in the Lord and still do well,
Within the land securely dwell,
Feed on His faithfulness;....
Yea, to the Lord thy way is known;
Confide in Him, Who on the throne
Abides in power divine;
Thy righteousness He shall display;
Resplendent as the light of day,
It shall unclouded shine.

—Psalter 95, Psalm 37

# God Called Abraham

*When Abram was ninety-nine years old, the LORD appeared to Abram, and said to him, "I am Almighty God, walk before me and be blameless. And I will make My covenant between Me and you, and will multiply you exceedingly." Then Abram fell on his face and God talked with him, saying, "As for Me, behold, My covenant is with you, and you shall be a father of many nations. No longer shall your name be called Abram, but your name shall be Abraham, for I have made you a father of many nations"* (Genesis 17:1-5).

God emphasized that this covenant would be everlasting, and that as a permanent sign of this covenant, Abraham and his descendants were to circumcise all eight-day-old baby boys. God went on to say that the covenant would not only apply to Abraham's descendants, but also to his slaves and servants who lived with him (Genesis 17:11-14, 23). It was to be an inclusive, not an exclusive, covenant. Also, it was not optional, but obligatory.

During the Second World War, to be circumcised was a death sentence in Nazi-occupied countries. In spite of this fact, most Jews continued to circumcise their baby boys on the eighth day, obedient to God's command to Abraham, because God's covenant with Abraham is an everlasting covenant (Genesis 17:19).

> O praise the Lord, His deeds make known
> And call upon His Name;
> Sing ye to Him, His praises sing,
> His wondrous works proclaim….
>
> Seek ye Jehovah and His strength,
> Seek Him forevermore.
>
> Ye children of God's covenant,
> Who of His grace have heard;
> Forget not all His wondrous deeds
> And judgments of His word.
>
> —Psalter 289, Psalm 105

# God Reaffirms Isaac

*And the LORD appeared to him* [Isaac] *the same night and said, "I am the God of your father Abraham; do not fear for I am with you. I will bless you and multiply your descendants, for my servant Abraham's sake."*

*So he* [Isaac] *built an altar there and called on the name of the LORD, and he pitched his tent there; and there Isaac's servants dug a well* (Genesis 26:24, 25).

After a series of unsuccessful attempts to dig wells to supply his flocks, and having those wells seized from them by herdsmen of Gerar, God spoke to Isaac and reaffirmed the covenant He had made with Abraham, Isaac's father. And this time the herdsmen of Gerar did not challenge the ownership of the well.

The reason Abimelech gave for requesting a covenant with Isaac was, "We have certainly seen that the LORD is with you, so we said, let there now be an oath between us.... You are now the blessed of the LORD' (Genesis 26:28, 29).

The pagans from the land of Canaan had noticed the God was blessing Isaac, and that a good relationship with him promised them a share in these blessings. A life of obedience to the Lord also blesses those around us.

In songs of sublime adoration and praise
Ye pilgrims, for Zion who press,
Break forth and extol the great Ancient of Days,
For His rich and distinguishing grace.

His love from eternity fixed upon you
Broke forth and uncovered its flame,
When each with the cords of His kindness He drew,
And brought you to love His great Name.

What was there in you that could merit esteem,
Or give the Creator delight?
'Twas "even so, Father," you ever must sing,
"Because it seemed good in Thy sight."

—Keen?

# God Affirms His Covenant with Jacob

*Now Jacob went out from Beersheba and went toward Haran…. Then he dreamed, and behold, a ladder was set up on the earth, and its top reached to heaven, and there the angels of God were ascending and descending on it, and behold, the LORD stood above it and said, "I am the LORD God of Abraham your father and the God of Isaac; the land on which you lie I will give to you and your descendants…."* (Genesis 28:10, 12, 13).

When God affirmed His covenant with Abraham and Isaac, He affirmed it with men who were esteemed righteous by their contemporaries. But when He affirmed it with Jacob, it was with a man who had to flee from his home, because he had cheated his twin brother of his birthright by deceiving his blind father.

Come, thou Fount of every blessing,
Tune my heart to sing Thy praise;
Streams of mercy, never ceasing,
Call for songs of loudest praise.
Teach me some melodious sonnet,
Sung by flaming tongues above:
Praise the Mount, I'm fixed upon it,
Mount of Thy redeeming love.

Here I raise my Ebenezer,
Hither by Thy help I'm come;
And I hope, by Thy good pleasure,
Safely to arrive at home.
Jesus sought me when a stranger,
Wandering from the fold of God;
He, to rescue me from danger,
Interposed His precious blood.

O to grace how great a debtor,
Daily I'm constrained to be;
Let Thy goodness, like a fetter,
Bind my wandering heart to Thee.

—Robert Robertson

# Joseph: a Models Righteousness

*The LORD was with Joseph, and he was a successful man; and he was in the house of his master* [Potiphar] *the Egyptian. And his master saw that the LORD was with him and that the LORD made all he did to prosper in his hand* (Genesis 39:2, 3).

[Joseph refused to lie with Potiphar's wife:] *"How then can I do this great wickedness and sin against God?"* (Genesis 39:9).

Joseph was Jacob's favorite son, because he was the oldest son of his favorite wife, Rachel. Unlike his father Jacob, Joseph was a God-fearing youth, who never forgot his early training after he was rejected by his brothers and sold as a slave in Egypt.

When he confronted his cruel brothers years later, he was able to forgive them and say, "But now, do not therefore be grieved or angry with yourselves because you sold me here, for God sent me before you to preserve life…So now it was not you who sent me here, but God, and He has made me a father to Pharaoh, and lord of all his house, and a ruler throughout all the land of Egypt" (Genesis 45:5, 7, 8).

In many ways Joseph is a pattern of godliness that we should imitate, and he is also a figure of Christ, who suffered for others' sins and did not avenge himself, but showed love to those who had abused him. In many ways a contrast to his father, who conspired to cheat his blind father and his twin brother.

How shall the young direct their way?
What light shall be their perfect guide?
Thy word, O Lord, shall safely lead,
If in its wisdom they confide.

Sincerely have I sought Thee, Lord,
O let me not from Thee depart;
To know Thy will and keep from sin,
Give me an understanding heart.

—Psalter 322, Psalm 119

## Moses: "I Drew Him out of the Water."

*And when she* [Pharaoh's daughter] *opened it* [the little ark-basket], *she saw the child, and behold, the baby wept. So she had compassion on him, and said, "This is one of the Hebrews' children." Then his sister* [Miriam] *said to Pharaoh's daughter, "Shall I go and call a nurse for you from the Hebrew women, that she may nurse the child for you?" And Pharaoh's daughter said to her, "Go." So the maiden went and called the child's mother* (Exodus 2: 6-8).

Earlier in the story Pharaoh had summoned the Hebrew midwives to order them that they must kill at birth any boy-babies they delivered. They replied that this was impossible, since the Hebrew women were very vigorous. Then they simply ignored his edict, and the result was that God blessed them (Exodus 1:18-21).

God worked out His purposes through a member of Pharaoh's own family: his daughter. He prepared a deliverer for His people through a baby saved from the selective holocaust.

Jochebed was granted the privilege of caring for her own baby until he was weaned, probably until he attained six or seven years of age. Not only could she care for him and teach him, but she was even paid a stipend to do so.

"O the depths of the wisdom and knowledge of God! How unsearchable are His judgments and His ways past finding out" (Romans 11:13)!

God moves in a mysterious way His wonders to perform;
He plants His footsteps in the sea, and rides upon the storm.

Ye fearful saints, fresh courage take,
The clouds ye so much dread
Are big with mercy and will break in blessings on your head.

Blind unbelief is sure to err, and scan His work in vain;
God is His own interpreter, and He will make it plain.

—William Cowper

# Joshua's Call

*Moses my servant is dead. Now, therefore, arise, go over the Jordan, you and the people, to the land which I am giving to them—the children of Israel....*

*No man shall be able to stand before you all the days of your life. As I was with Moses, so I will be with you. I will not forsake you.... Only be strong and very courageous, that you may observe to do according to all the law which my servant Moses commanded you. Do not turn from it to the right or to the left, that you may prosper wherever you go. This book of the law shall not depart from your mouth, but you shall meditate in it day and night...* (Joshua 1:2, 5, 7).

The Lord made very clear what is the recipe for successfully living for Him. It is to "meditate day and night" on God's Word, and to keep it in constant focus.

Dear friend, He may not call us to lead people to a "promised land," as He did Joshua, but He has called us to "love the LORD our God, that we may obey His voice, and that we may cling to Him, for He is our life and the length of our days" (Deuteronomy 30:20).

As we near the end of our pilgrimage on earth, we need to renew our pledge to love the LORD our God and meditate on His Word day and night.

Open my eyes that I may see
Glimpses of truth Thou hast for me;
Place in my hand the wonderful key
That shall unclasp and set me free.
Silently now I wait for Thee; ready my God Thy will to see;
Open my eyes, illumine me, Spirit divine.

Open my ears that I may hear
Voices of truth Thou sendest clear;
And while the wave-notes fall on my ear,
Everything false will disappear.

—Charles H. Scott

# God Sends a Woman to Judge Israel

*Now Deborah, a prophetess, the wife of Lapidoth, was judging Israel at that time.... Then she sent and called for Barak the son of Abinoam ... and said to him, "Has not the LORD God of Israel commanded, 'Go and deploy troops at Mount Tabor; take with you ten thousand men of the sons of Naphtali and of the sons of Zebulon; and against you I will deploy Sisera, the commander of Jabin's army, with his chariots and his multitude at the River Kishon, and I will deliver him into your hand"*(Judges 4:4, 5-7)?

When Deborah called Barak to task, he refused to obey God's command unless Deborah would go with him. She consented to do so, but warned him that when God delivered the enemy leader into their hands, a woman would get the credit instead of Barak.

Sometimes God accepts our conditional obedience, but not always. We know He accepted Jacob's conditional obedience without question at Bethel, but in Barak's case He did not.

When Sisera fled from the advancing Israelite troops, he took refuge with Jael, a Canaanite woman. She took him into her tent and gave him milk to drink and a place to rest. After he was asleep she drove a tent peg into his temple with a hammer and killed him.

The fifth chapter of Judges is devoted to Deborah's song of praise to the Lord for the victory.

I look not back; God knows the fruitless efforts,
The wasted years, the sinning, the regrets;
I leave them all with Him who blots the record,
And graciously forgives, and then forgets.

I look not forward, God sees all the future;
The road that short or long will lead me home;
And He will face with me its every trial,
And bear for me the burdens that may come.

But I look up into the face of Jesus,
For there my heart can rest, my fears are stilled;....

—Annie Johnson Flint

# God Calls Gideon

*And the Angel of the LORD appeared to him [Gideon], and said to him, "The LORD is with you, you mighty man of valor!"*

*Gideon said to Him, "O my lord, if the LORD is with us, why then has all this happened to us? And where are all His miracles which our fathers told us about, saying, 'Did not the LORD bring us up from Egypt?' But now the LORD has forsaken us and delivered us into the hands of the Midianites."*

*Then the LORD turned to him and said, "Go in this might of yours and you shall save Israel from the hand of the Midianites. Have I not sent you"* (Judges 6:12-14)?

Gideon then reminded God how unimportant he was. He described his group as "being the weakest clan in Manasseh, and himself as the least in his father's house" (Judges 6:15). God replied that He would be with him and promised he would "defeat the Midianites as one man" (Judges 6:16).

Gideon tested his call three times, and then summoned warriors from four tribes to engage the Midianite army. God whittled Gideon's army of 32,000 down to 300 men, so that He alone would receive the glory. Gideon armed his troops with trumpets and torches carried in pitchers, and they shouted, "The sword of the LORD and of Gideon!" The Midianites fled and God granted the Israelites a great victory.

> The Lord Almighty is my light; He is my Savior ever near,
> And since my strength is in His might,
> Who can distress me or affright,
> What evil shall I fear?
>
> My heart had failed in fear and woe, unless in God I had believed,
> Assured that He would mercy show,
> And that my life His grace would know,
> Nor was my hope deceived....
>
> Be strong, nor be thy heart dismayed,
> Wait and the Lord will bring thee aid. Yea, trust and never fear.
>
> —Psalter 73, Psalm 27

# Ruth, the Moabitess

*Both the daughters of Lot were with child by their father. The firstborn bore a son, and called his name Moab; he is the father of the Moabites to this day* (Genesis 19:36, 37).

[Naomi's sons] *took wives of the women of Moab; the name of the one was Orpah, and the name of the other Ruth...* (Ruth 1:4).

*Salmon begot Boaz by Rahab, Boaz begot Obed by Ruth, and Obed begot Jesse, and Jesse begot David the king* (Matthew 1:5, 6).

The book of Ruth does not reveal the name of Boaz' mother, but only the name of his father [Salmon], as does the Gospel of Luke in his genealogy (chapter 3), but the Gospel of Matthew's review of the messianic line spells out her name clearly. Rahab was the harlot of Jericho, who sheltered the Israelite spies because she believed in the power of their God (Hebrews 11:31). Because of her faith, she and her father's family were saved when Jericho was invaded. The Bible is silent about the influence she may have exercised on Boaz because of her history, but it is possible that he was favorably inclined toward Ruth because she was another Gentile who believed in Israel's God.

The history of two Gentile women in the messianic line reminds us that God never excluded the Gentiles from His gracious purposes.

Praise ye the Lord, for He is good;
Give thanks and bless His name;
His lovingkindness changes not, from age to age the same.

What tongue can tell His mighty deeds,
His wondrous works and ways?
O who can show His glory forth, or utter all His praise?

O Lord, remember me in grace, let me salvation see;
The grace Thou showest to Thy saints, that grace reveal to me.

—Psalter 290, Psalm 106

# Hannah: She Lent Her Son to God

*Hannah conceived and bore a son, and called his name Samuel, saying, "Because I have asked for him from the LORD"....*

*Now the man Elkanah and all his house went up to offer to the LORD the yearly sacrifice,,,, But Hannah did not go up, for she said to her husband, "Not until the child is weaned, then I will take him, that he may appear before the LORD and remain there forever"* (1 Samuel 1:20b-22).

*And the LORD visited Hannah, so that she conceived and bore three sons and two daughters. Meanwhile the child Samuel grew before the LORD* (1 Samuel 2:21).

In the first chapter we meet Hannah, who is grieving because she has no child. She goes to the temple to pour out her heart to God, and goes home again, comforted. In due time, God blesses Hannah as she conceives. Then she resolves—as an act of worship—that she will "lend the child to the Lord for his entire life," and does so. At this point she is unsure whether she will ever have another child, but is faithful to her resolve to bring him to live in the temple when he is weaned.

Dear friend, have you been faithful to keep the promise you made to God when you were in despair? Hannah reaped the blessings of her obedience and had five more children.

Hushed was the evening hymn, the temple courts were dark,
The lamp was burning dim before the sacred ark,
When suddenly a voice divine
Rang through the silence of the shrine.

The old man, meek and mild, the priest of Israel, slept;
His watch: the temple-child, the little Levite kept.
And what from Eli's sense was sealed,
The Lord to Hannah's son revealed.

O give me Samuel's mind, a sweet, unmurmuring faith,
Obedient and resigned to Thee in life and death.

—James D. Burns

# God Calls a Shepherd Boy

*Now the LORD said to Samuel, "How long will you mourn for Saul, seeing I have rejected him from reigning over Israel? Fill your horn with oil and go. I am sending you to Jesse the Behlehemite, for I have provided Myself a king among his sons"* (1 Samuel 16:1).

*But David said to Saul, "Your servant used to keep his father's sheep, and when a lion or a bear came and took a lamb out of the flock, I went out after it and struck it, and delivered the lamb from its mouth, and when it rose against me, I caught it by its beard and struck and killed it"* (1 Samuel 17:34, 35).

Saul had seemed like such a good choice for Israel's first king. He was strikingly tall and apparently a humble young man, since he was shy to broadcast the fact that God had chosen him to be king of Israel. Yet after he had worn the crown for a short while he decided that he need not follow God's specific instructions, but made his own rules. He was a major disappointment to God and His prophet Samuel.

When Samuel obediently went to anoint the one who would succeed Saul from among Jesse's tall sons, he found that young David's family didn't think much of his capabilities. They saw only the boyishness of the youngest son, yet God saw a heart that was ardent with love for his Shepherd. David sang:

The Lord's my Shepherd, I'll not want,
He makes me down to lie
In pastures green, He leadeth me the quiet waters by.

My soul He doth restore again,
And me to walk doth make
Within the paths of righteousness e'en for His own Name's sake.

Goodness and mercy all my life
Shall surely follow me;
And in God's house forevermore my dwelling place shall be.

—Psalter 53, Psalm 23

# God Chooses Solomon

[The prophet Nathan urged Bathsheba,] *Go immediately to King David and say to him, 'Did you not, my lord, O king, swear to your maidservant, saying, "Assuredly your son Solomon shall reign after me, and he shall sit on my throne"* (1 Kings 1:13)*?*

*Then God said to him* [Solomon], *"Because you have asked this thing* [wisdom]*, and have not asked long life for yourself, nor have asked riches for yourself, nor have asked the life of your enemies, but have asked for yourself understanding to discern justice, behold I have done according to your words....* (1 Kings 3:11, 12a).

It is interesting to note that God did not choose Solomon because of his unique wisdom, but that He chose him because He loved his father David, and then endowed him with unique wisdom, and added riches, longevity, and political ascendency.

Solomon began his reign with everything in his favor (1 Kings 3:3). Unhappily, he ended his reign on a more negative note. He had been sidetracked by his many wives and concubines, and led into idolatry (1 Kings 11:1-12).

It is not enough to begin well; we also need to finish well. The hymn writer emphasized this:

Awake, my soul, stretch every nerve
And press with vigor on;
A heavenly race demands thy zeal,
And an immortal crown.

A cloud of witnesses around
Hold thee in full survey;
Forget the steps already trod,
And onward urge thy way.

Blest Savior, introduced by Thee,
Have I my race begun;
And crowned with victory, at Thy feet
I'll lay my honors down.

—Philip Doddridge

# God Singles Out Jeroboam's Son

Ahijah, the blind prophet, was sent with this message to Jeroboam's wife: *Arise therefore, go to your own house. When your feet enter the city, the child shall die. And all Israel shall mourn for him and bury him, for he is the only one of Jeroboam who shall come to the grave, because in him there is found something good toward the LORD God of Israel in the house of Jeroboam* (1 Kings 14:12, 13).

Jeroboam, the first king of the divided northern kingdom, had introduced the worship of a golden calf in an attempt to prevent his people from going to the temple in the southern kingdom to worship God. When his child was critically ill, he sent his wife to the southern kingdom in disguise to beseech the aging prophet— Ahijah— to heal him.

Although Ahijah was blind, he had discerned the woman's identity, and pronounced God's judgment on Jeroboam and his descendants. Yet this sick child's heart was tender towards the God of Israel, and his death was God's evidence of special mercy toward him. He was the only one of Jeroboam's descendants to be honored with a national memorial funeral, and God spared him the experience of suffering with his family (Isaiah 57:1, 2). "Precious in the sight of the LORD is the death of His saints" (Psalm 116:15).

> Lo, such the child whose early feet
> The paths of peace have trod;
> Whose secret heart with influence sweet
> Is upward drawn to God.
>
> And soon, too soon, the wintry hour
> Of man's maturer age,
> Will shake the soul with sorrow's power,
> And stormy passions rage.
>
> Dependant on Thy bounteous breath,
> We seek Thy grace alone
> In childhood, manhood, age, and death,
> To keep us still Thine own.

—Reginald Heber

# Elijah, God's Prophet

*And Elijah the Tishbite, of the inhabitants of Gilead, said to Ahab, "As the LORD God of Israel lives, before whom I stand, there shall not be dew nor rain these years, except at my word."*

*Then the word of the LORD came to him [Elijah], saying, "Get away from here and turn eastward, and hide by the brook Cherith, which flows into the Jordan. And it will be that you shall drink from the brook, and I have commanded the ravens to feed you there"* (1 Kings 17:1-4).

The history of the northern kingdom reveals a list of ungodly kings. In Elijah's day the king was Ahab. The record says: "And it came to pass, as though it had been a trivial things for him to walk in the sins of Jeroboam the son of Nebat, that he took as wife Jezebel, the daughter of Ethbaal, king of the Sidonians, and he went and served Baal and worshiped him" (1 Kings 16:31).

James wrote: "Elijah was a man with a nature like ours, and he prayed earnestly that it would not rain, and it did not rain on the land for three years and six months. And he prayed again and the heaven gave rain, and the earth produced its fruit" (James 5:17, 18). Elijah also appeared with Moses during Christ's transfiguration, in the final days of His earthly ministry to encourage Him as He faced His crucifixion death (Luke 9:30, 31). Elijah was the second of only two men who were taken to heaven without passing through death (2 Kings 2:11).

> Springs and streams no longer bless
> All the dry and thirsty land;
> Fertile fields in verdant dress
> God converts to desert sands,
> For that those who dwell therein
> Turn to wickedness and sin.
>
> When His righteous judgments come,
> Strong to bless and to destroy,
> All iniquity is dumb,
> All the righteous sing for joy.
>
> —Psalter 296, Psalm 107

# God Consecrates Elisha

[God gave Elijah His final orders:] *"Also you shall anoint Jehu the son of Nimshi as king over Israel. And Elisha the son of Shaphat of Abel Meholah you shall anoint as prophet in your place." So he departed from there, and found Elisha the son of Shaphat, who was plowing with twelve yoke of oxen before him, and he was with the twelfth. Then Elijah passed by him and threw his mantle on him* (1 Kings 19:16).

When God called Elisha to take over Elijah's ministry of prophecy to the kingdom of Israel, Elisha was well aware that there would be few lasting effects of being God's mouthpiece to the wicked and idolatrous kings. Yet he faithfully carried out his mandate even when his life was threatened and refused all kinds of remuneration for his ministry. The chronicles of the Kings are replete with the miracles Elisha performed under God's commands. I have not tallied them, but I believe that he was enabled to perform more miracles during his tenure that his more dramatic predecessor Elijah had done.

May God grant us the grace to obey God's commands as whole-heartedly as did both Elijah and Elisha.

He leads us on by paths we did not know;
Upward He leads us, though our steps be slow;
He leads us on through all the unquiet years;
Past all our dreamland hopes and doubts and fears.
He guides our steps through all the tangled maze,
Of losses, sorrows, and o'erclouded days;
We know His will is done, and still He leads us on.

And soon or late the rugged field of strife
Shall catch the sunlight that transfigures life;
The heart shall win the disciplines of pain,
And know the struggle has not been in vain.
The doubts and fears shall cease,
And Christ will bring it peace.

—Hiram O. Riley, vs. 1 and 2; vs. 3, written later

# A Little Slave-Girl Testifies

*The Syrians had gone out on raids and had brought back captive a young girl from the land of Israel. She waited on Naaman's wife.*

*Then she said to her mistress, "If only my master were with the prophet who is in Samaria! For he would heal him of his leprosy"* (2 Kings 5:2, 3).

We are given no details about this little maid, only that she had been stolen from her home back in Israel, and served as a slave in the household of Naaman, a military chief. We do know that she was a worshiper of Israel's God and that she had a tender heart. She was concerned for the dilemma in which Naaman found himself when he developed the crippling disease of leprosy. She knew that God could heal him, and urged her mistress to let her master know how he could be healed.

The Syrian soldiers had taken the maiden away from all that was dear and familiar, but they had not been able to taken away her faith in YAWEH. She carried His Name in her heart.

Dear friend, remember to carry His Name in your heart, wherever you go.

> Take the Name of Jesus with you,
> Child of sorrow and of woe;
> It will joy and comfort give you,
> Take it then where e'er you go.
>
> Take the Name of Jesus ever
> As a shield from every snare;
> If temptations round you gather,
> Breathe that holy Name in prayer.
>
> O the precious Name of Jesus,
> How it thrills our souls with joy
> When His loving arms receive us,
> And His songs our tongues employ.
>
> —Mrs. Lydia Baxter

# The Princess Who Saved the Infant King

*When Athaliah the mother of Ahaziah saw that her son was dead, she arose and destroyed all the royal heirs. But Jehosheba, the daughter of King Joram, sister of Ahaziah, took Joash the son of Ahaziah, and stole him away from among the king's sons who were being murdered, and they hid him and his nurse in the bedroom from Athaliah, so that he was not killed. So he was hidden with her in the house of the LORD for six years, while Athaliah reigned over the land* (2 Kings 11:1-3).

Our attention now is turned to the southern kingdom (Judah) where Athaliah, the daughter of Ahab and Jezebel had seized the throne after her son (Ahaziah) was killed by Jehu, who carried out God's vengeance on the ungodly family of Ahab. Athaliah seems to have been as cruel as her mother Jezebel, in that she killed all her royal grandsons in order to take over the rule of Judah.

Jehosheba was married to the high priest Jehoiada who took upon himself the responsibility to raise the future king of Judah (also called "Jehoash") in the fear and admonition of God (2 Kings 12:2). As long as the high priest lived, the young king faithfully worshiped God. He was anointed king of Judah after he was weaned, when he was seven years old.

This royal aunt was God's instrument in keeping His promise to David that his descendants would ever sit on his throne.

Thou, O Lord, art God alone, everlasting is Thy throne;
Through the ages men shall sing praise to heaven's eternal King.
Thou, enthroned above the skies, wilt for Zion's help arise.
Let Thy grace to her appear, for the promised time is near.

This all ages shall record for the glory of the Lord;
Thou dost hear the humble prayer, for the helpless Thou dost care;
Thou eternal art and great, heaven and earth Thou didst create,
Heaven and earth shall pass away,
Changeless Thou shalt live for aye.

—Psalter 275, Psalm 102

# Isaiah, a Prophet of Comfort

[Isaiah wrote:] *Then one of the seraphim flew to me, having in his hand a live coal, which he had taken with tongs from the altar, and he touched my mouth with it, and said, "Behold, this has touched your lips; your iniquity is taken away, and your sin purged." Also I heard the voice of the Lord, saying, "Whom shall I send, and who will go for Us?" Then I said, "Here am I! Send me"* (Isaiah 6:6-8).

*"Comfort, yes, comfort My people!" says your God. "Speak comfort to Jerusalem, and cry out to her that her warfare is ended, that her iniquity is pardoned, for she has received from the LORD's hand double for all her sins" (Isaiah 40:1, 2).*

The first thirty-nine chapters of Isaiah's prophecy deal with mostly contemporary issues, although it also contains messianic promises. The final 27 chapters have been dubbed "the book of comfort." In it we find many promises dealing with the messianic age and the age to come. God said: "It is too small a thing that You should be My Servant to raise up the tribes of Jacob, ... I will also give You as a light to the Gentiles that You should be My salvation to the ends of the earth" (Isaiah 49:6).

Hear the Lord of harvest sweetly calling,
"Who will go and work for Me today?
Who will bring to Me the lost and dying?
Who will point them to the narrow way?"

When the coal of fire touched the prophet,
Making him as pure, as pure can be,
When the voice of God said, "Who'll go for us?"
Then he answered, "Here am I, send me."

Millions now in sin and shame are dying,
Listen to their sad and bitter cry;
Hasten, brother, hasten to the rescue;
Quickly answer, "Master, here am I."

—George Bennard

# Jeremiah, the Weeping Prophet

[Jeremiah said,] *Righteous are You, O LORD, when I plead with You; yet let me talk with You about Your judgments. Why does the way of the wicked prosper? Why are those happy who deal so treacherously? You have planted them, yes, they have taken root, they grow, yes, they bear fruit. You are near to their mouth, but far from their mind* (Jeremiah 12:1, 2).

*You have moved my soul far from peace; I have forgotten prosperity, and I said, "My strength and my hope have perished from the LORD.... My soul still remembers and sinks within me"* (Lamentations 3:17, 18, 20).

Jeremiah lived during a chaotic time in the life of the kingdom of Judah. He was a teenager when God called him to carry His warnings of coming judgment to the people, who resented this young man for saying what no one wanted to hear or believe. As the storm clouds darkened the proverbial sky, he suffered along with the people and in addition became the target of their resentment. The world has not changed. We still don't like bad news and we resent those who insist on repeating it. The sons of Korah sang a psalm that could have been Jeremiah's complaint:

Lord, the God of my salvation,
Day and night I cry to Thee;
Let my prayer now find acceptance
In Thy mercy, answer me.
Full of trouble and affliction,
Nigh to death my soul is brought;
Helpless, like one cast forever
From Thy care and from Thy thought.

Thou hast brought me down to darkness,
'Neath Thy wrath I am oppressed;
All the billows of affliction
Overwhelm my soul distressed.
Thou hast made my friends despise me,
And companionless I go;...

—Psalter 240, Psalm 88

# Ezekiel, the Priest-Prophet

[Ezekiel wrote:] *Now it came to pass in the thirtieth year, in the fourth month, on the fifth day of the month, as I was among the captives by the River of Chebar, that the heavens were opened and I saw visions of God. On the fifth day of the month, which was the fifth year of King Jehoiachin's captivity, the word of the LORD came expressly to Ezekiel the priest, the son of Buzi, in the land of the Chaldeans by the River Chebar, and the hand of the LORD was upon him there* (Ezekiel 1:1-3).

God called the priest Ezekiel—now a captive himself—to bring His word to the captives who had been forcibly dragged to Babylon. Unlike Isaiah and Jeremiah, who also prophesied during this period, Ezekiel was shown many visions. His instructions were: "I am sending you to them, and you shall say to them, 'Thus says the Lord God.' As for them, whether they hear or whether they refuse—for they are a rebellious house—they will know that a prophet has been among them" (Ezekiel 2:4b, 5).

When God called Ezekiel as His prophet, he reminded him that he was not guaranteed a responsive audience. He needed to be prepared for resentment and even open rebellion. "They are a rebellious house," God reminded him. We cannot expect all those to whom we witness to be responsive. Some will even refuse our message and hate us.

> Lord, hear my prayer, and let my cry
> Have ready access unto thee;
> When in distress to Thee I fly,
> O hide not Thou Thy face from me.
> Attend, O Lord, to my desire,
> O haste to answer when I pray;
> For grief consumes my strength like fire,
> My days as smoke pass swift away.
>
> My heart is withered like the grass,
> And I forget my daily bread;
> In lonely grief my days I pass
> And sad my thoughts upon my bed.

—Psalter 272, Psalm 102

# Daniel, the Righteous

*The king instructed* [the chief eunuch to bring] *some of the children of Israel and some of the king's descendants and some of the nobles, young men in whom there was no blemish, but good-looking, gifted in wisdom, possessing knowledge and quick to understand, who had ability to serve in the king's palace, and whom they might teach the language and literature of the Chaldeans.... Now from among those of the sons of Judah were Daniel, Hananiah, Mishael, and Azariah. To them the ... eunuch gave names: Belteshazzar,... Shadrach, ... Meshach, and ... Abednego* (Daniel 1:3-7).

All four young men were gifted and God-fearing, but Daniel became outstanding in that he had the gift of interpreting visions and dreams. The book of Daniel is the last of the major prophets, and theologians are still debating the meanings of the future-oriented prophesies.

All four of these young men were faithful servants of the God of their fathers, and consequently refused to worship the idols of the pagans among whom they lived. The three young men— Shadrach, Meshach, and Abednego—violated a universal law requiring that everyone was to worship an image whenever a horn was blown. They politely defied the king, and the sentence was carried out, but the observers noted that four men—not three— walked freely about in the flames, unhurt (Daniel 3).

Daniel was the specific target of his competitors who wanted to eliminate him, so they trapped him into defying the king's order to cease praying to anyone but the king. He defied that edict, and was thrown into a lion's den. God protected His servant by shutting the lions' mouths (Daniel 6).

Standing by a purpose true, heeding God's command,
Honor them, the faithful few, all hail to Daniel's band!

Many mighty men are lost, daring not to stand
Who for God had been a host by joining Daniel's band!

—Philip P. Bliss

# God Calls Hosea

*The word of the LORD that came to Hosea the son of Beeri, in the days of Uzziah, Jotham, Ahaz, and Hezekiah, kings of Judah, and in the days of Jeroboam the son of Joash, king of Israel. When the LORD began to speak by Hosea, the LORD said to Hosea: "Go, take yourself a wife of harlotry, and children of harlotry, for the land has committed great harlotry by departing from the LORD"* (Hosea 1:1-2).

God called Hosea before Assyria had invaded Israel and before Babylon had invaded Judah to drag the populace captive to other countries. God was still calling the people to repentance in order to forestall His divine judgment. Isaiah was given verbal messages to the Israelites, Jeremiah revealed God's grief over the rebellion of His people, Ezekiel was given visions to share, while Daniel received dreams. But Hosea had to live out the metaphor of a people who were unfaithful to God by taking a harlot as a wife.

Yet God urged the unfaithful nation to repent and return to Him: "Sow for yourselves righteousness, reap in mercy; break up your fallow ground. For it is time to seek the LORD, till He comes and rains righteousness upon you" (Hosea 10:12).

The other "minor prophets" also reveal a God who is holy and who cannot tolerate wickedness, yet He is a God who is merciful and reluctant to punish the wicked as they deserve.

Though faint, yet pursuing, we go on our way,
The Lord is our Leader, His word is our stay;
Though suffering and sorrow, and trial be near,
The Lord is our Refuge, and whom can we fear?

He raiseth the fallen, He cheereth the faint,
The weak and oppressed, He will hear their complaint;
The way may be weary, and thorny the road,
But how can we falter? Our help is the Lord.

The clouds may surround us, our God is our light;
Though storms rage around us, our God is our might.

—Anonymous

# God Is Merciful and Just

*Mercy and truth have met together, righteousness and peace have kissed. Truth shall spring out of the earth, and righteousness shall look down from heaven* (Psalm 85:10, 11).

*In Him we have redemption through His blood, the forgiveness of sins, according to the riches of His grace which He made to abound toward us in all wisdom and prudence.... God, who is rich in mercy, because of His great love with which He loved us, even when we were dead in trespasses, made us alive together with Christ (by grace you have been saved)....* (Ephesians 1:7; 2:4, 5).

As we peruse the "minor prophets" we have glimpses of God's wrath against the people's sins, and His yearning for them to repent and return to Him so that He need not punish them as they deserved. We can even see that He pronounced judgment on the pagan nations that cruelly assaulted the Hebrew people, although He permitted them to execute His judgment on the rebellious Israelites.

We may understand a righteous God, or even approve of a merciful God, but we do not understand a God who is both just and merciful. But in reading the New Testament, we see that Jesus Christ took on our guilt during His incarnation, all the way to His death on the cross, so that we guilty sinners might be freed from our deserved condemnation.

Yea, the Lord is full of mercy and compassion for distress,
Slow to anger and abundant in His love and tenderness.
He will not be angry always, nor will He forever chide,
Though we oft have sinned against Him,
Still His love and grace abide.

As the heavens are high above us,
Great His love to us has proved,
Far as east from west is distant, He has all our sins removed.
As a father loves his children, feeling pity for their woes,
So the Lord to those that fear Him,
Mercy and compassion shows.

—Psalter 280, Psalm 103

# Grief for Divine Judgment

*Then I* [Daniel] *set my face toward the LORD God to make request by prayer and supplications, with fasting, sackcloth, and ashes, and I prayed to the LORD my God, and made confession, and said, "O God, great and awesome God, who keeps the covenant and mercy with those who love Him, and with those who keep His commandments; we have sinned and committed iniquity, we have done wickedly and rebelled, even by departing from Your precepts and Your judgments, neither have we heeded Your servants, the prophets, who spoke in Your name to our kings and princes, to our fathers, and to all the people of the land....* (Daniel 9:4-6).

Here Daniel—although personally faithful and God-fearing— set us a pattern for a prayer of confession on behalf of a faithless, rebellious nation, of which he was a member. His prayer stands in vivid contrast to the hypocritical prayer of the Pharisee, whose prayer pointed out to God how superior he was to the socially-despised publican (Luke 18:9-14).

Dear friend, it is fitting that we should confess the sins of the society of which we are members. Although we may not be actively guilty of all its sins, we often derive benefits from the oppression of the underprivileged classes of our society.

> Lord, rebuke me not in anger,
> Chastened sore, I waste away;
> Pity my distress and hear me,
> Lord, how long wilt Thou delay?
>
> Pity, Lord, my sad condition,
> I am weary and distressed;
> Many adversaries vex me,
> Weeping, I can find no rest.
>
> Now the foes that seek to harm me,
> Quickly put to shame, shall flee—
> For the Lord has heard my weeping,
> And He will regard my plea.
>
> —Psalter 12, Psalm 6

# Jerusalem's Agony

*How lonely sits the city that was full of people! How like a widow is she, who was great among the nations! The princess among the provinces has become a slave!... All her friends have dealt treacherously with her; they have become her enemies....*

*Judah has gone into captivity, under affliction and hard servitude..... Her adversaries have become the master, her enemies prosper. For the LORD has afflicted her because of the multitude of her transgressions* (Lamentations 1:1, 2b, 3a, 5).

Jeremiah penned his lament over the fall of Jerusalem, as God's long-delayed judgment fell on the rebellious nation. Yet even as the beautiful city was razed of its fabulous architecture, God promised to restore the nation after seventy years of banishment, and Jeremiah was comforted (see Lamentations 3:21-33).

These same verses have comforted God's children down through the ages as they faced devastation and ruin: "This I recall to mind, and therefore I have hope: through the LORD's mercies we are not consumed, because His compassions fail not. They are new every morning; great is Your faithfulness. The LORD is my portion, says my soul, therefore I hope in Him! The LORD is good to those who wait for Him, to the soul that seeks Him."

An unknown psalmist sang:

> By Babel's streams we sat and wept,
> For memory still to Zion clung;
> The wind alone our harp strings swept,
> That on the drooping willows hung.

> Not songs but sighs to us belong when Zion's walls in ruin lie;
> How shall we sing Jehovah's song,
> While in an alien land we die?

> O Zion fair, God's holy hill,
> Wherein our God delights to dwell,
> Let my right hand forget her skill, if I forget to love her well.

—Psalter 379, Psalm 137

# Habakkuk's Prayer and Testimony

The prophet prayed: *O LORD, I have heard Your speech and was afraid. O LORD, revive Your work in the midst of the years! In the midst of the years make it known; in wrath remember mercy* (Habakkuk 3:2).

As God's judgment fell on the rebellious nation of Judah, the faithful prophet quailed at the violence of the destruction of Jerusalem and the cruel suffering of the starving population as they were herded to Babylon as slaves. Seeing the cruelty of the invading Babylonians, he appealed to God's justice: "You are of purer eyes than to behold evil, and cannot look on wickedness; why do You look on those who deal treacherously, and hold Your tongue when the wicked devours a person more righteous than he" (Habakkuk 1:13)?

God replied, "Write the vision and make it plain on tablets that he may run who reads it. For the vision is yet for an appointed time, but in the end it will speak, and it will not lie. Though it tarries, wait for it, because it will surely come, it will not tarry. Behold the proud. His soul is not upright in him, but the just shall live by his faith" (Habakkuk 2:2-4).

Habakkuk closed his short (three chapters) book with his confession of faith, which rings triumphantly down the ages:

"Though the fig tree may not blossom, nor fruit be on the vines; though the labor of the olive may fail, and the fields yield no food; though the flock may be cut off from the fold, and there be no herd in the stalls—yet I will rejoice in the LORD, I will joy in the God of my salvation...." (Habakkuk 3:17, 18).

My griefs of heart abound; relieve my sore distress.
See my affliction and my pain, forgive my sinfulness.

Consider Thou my foes, so many and so bold.
For cruel is the hatred, Lord, which they against me hold.

Defend and keep my soul, from foes deliver me;
And let me not be brought to shame; I put my trust in Thee.

Psalter 63, Psalm 25

# John, the Baptizer

*The voice of one crying in the wilderness: "Prepare the way of the LORD. Make straight in the desert a highway for our God."* (Isaiah 40:3-5a).

*As is written in the prophets: "Behold, I send My messenger before Your face, who will prepare Your way before You. The voice of one crying in the wilderness: Prepare the way of the LORD; make His paths straight." John came baptizing in the wilderness and preaching a baptism of repentance for the remission of sins* (Mark 1:2-4).

John seems to have been the last of the Old Testament prophets, although he is not mentioned until the New Testament. His father Zachariah received the notice of his pending birth from the angel Gabriel as he was serving in the temple. John was the forerunner predicted by Isaiah (see above), and the angel announced that the baby boy would be "great in the sight of the Lord ... and be filled with the Holy Spirit, even from his mother's womb. And he will ... make ready a people prepared for the Lord" (Luke 1:15, 16, 17b).

John testified of Jesus: "Behold! The Lamb of God who takes away the sin of the world! This is He of whom I said, 'After me comes a Man who is preferred before me, for He was before me.' ... I have seen and testified that this is the Son of God" (John 1:29, 30, 34). John's entire life was spent as Messiah's forerunner (John 3:28). His rebuke of King Herod cost him his life. He was beheaded at the whims of an immoral woman and her young daughter (Mark 6:17-28).

Paschal Lamb, by God appointed, all our sins on Thee were laid;
    By almighty love anointed, Thou hast full atonement made.
All Thy people are forgiven, through the virtue of Thy blood;
Opened is the gate of heaven; peace is made 'twixt man and God.

—John Bakewell

# The Father Chooses and Adopts

*Blessed be God the Father of our Lord Jesus Christ, who has blessed us with every spiritual blessing in the heavenly places in Christ, just as He chose us in Him before the foundation of the world, that we should be holy and without blame before Him in love, having predestined us to adoption as sons by Jesus Christ to Himself, according to the good pleasure of His will, ...* (Ephesians 1:3-5).

In his letter to the church at Ephesus, Paul details all that our salvation entails. Not only does Christ's life and death restore the repentant sinner to Adam's first state—as fully acceptable to God, but by His death and resurrection He also provided us with a new status: that of children of God, and co-heirs with Christ.

The apostle John wrote: "He [Jesus] came to His own, and His own did not receive Him, but as many as received Him, to them He gave the right to become children of God, to those who believe in His name" (John 1:11, 12). He described the wonder of this adoption: "Behold, what manner of love the Father has bestowed on us, that we should be called children of God! ..... Beloved, now we are children of God, and it has not yet been revealed what we shall be, but we know that when He is revealed, we shall be like Him, for we shall see Him as He is" (1 John 3:1a, 2).

Dear friend, God did not adopt the angels, but He adopted sinners whom He has loved since before the foundation of the world!

How vast the benefits divine which we in Christ possess!
We're saved from guilt and every sin and called to holiness.

'Tis not for works which we have done, or shall hereafter do;
But He of His electing love, salvation doth bestow.

Our glorious Surety undertook redemption's wondrous plan;
And grace was given us in Him, before the world began.

Not one of all the chosen race but shall to heaven attain,
Partake on earth the purposed grace, and then with Jesus reign.

—Augustus M. Toplady

# The Son Unites through His Death

*In Him* [Jesus Christ] *we have redemption through His blood, the forgiveness of sins, according to the riches of His grace, which He made to abound toward us ..., that in the dispensation of the fullness of the times He might gather together in one all things in Christ, both which are in heaven and which are on earth—in Him* (Ephesians 1:7, 9, 10).

Solomon sang: "[Christ] shall have dominion from sea to sea, ... to the ends of the earth. Those who dwell in the wilderness will bow before Him.... Yes, all kings shall fall down before Him; all nations shall serve Him ... His name shall endure forever; His name shall continue as long as the sun, and ... all nations shall call Him blessed" (Psalm 72:7b-9, 17).

The apostle John had a vision of the Church Triumphant united with the celestial beings: "And they sang a new song, saying: 'You are worthy to take the scroll and to open the seals, for You were slain and have redeemed us to God by Your blood out of every tribe and tongue and people and nation" (Revelation 5:9, 10a).

Gone forever will be all the divisive labels of race, gender, class, language, and denominationalism. Jesus prayed, "I come to You, Holy Father; keep through Your name those You have given Me, that they may be one as We are" (John 17:11b).

The Church's one foundation is Jesus Christ her Lord;
She is His new creation by water and the word;
From heaven He came and sought her to be His holy bride;
With His own blood He bought her, and for her life He died.

Elect from every nation, yet one o'er all the earth,
Her charter of salvation: one Lord, one faith, one birth.
One holy name she blesses, partakes one holy food,
And to one hope she presses, with every grace endued.

Yet she on earth hath union with God, the Three-in-One,
And mystic, sweet communion with those whose rest is won; ...

—Samuel J. Stone

# The Holy Spirit Seals

*In Him* [Christ] *you also trusted, after you heard the word of truth, the gospel of your salvation; in whom also, having believed, you were sealed with the Holy Spirit of promise, who is the guarantee of our inheritance until the redemption of the purchased possession, to the praise of His glory* (Ephesians 1:13, 14).

[Paul also wrote to the church at Corinth:] *Now He who has prepared us for this very thing is God, who also has given us the Spirit as a guarantee"* (2 Corinthians 5:5).

It is the Holy Spirit who reassures us that we are God's children, and His working in our lives is a guarantee or earnest of our immortality and eternal life. The Holy Spirit makes God's word come alive and real to the sincere seeker, and thus empowers him to live a life of obedience to God.

When the religious leaders accused Jesus of serving the devil, He warned his critics: "I say to you, every sin and blasphemy will be forgiven men, but the blasphemy against the Spirit will not be forgiven men. Anyone who speaks a word against the Son of Man [Jesus], it will be forgiven him, but whoever speaks against the Holy Spirit, it will not be forgiven him, either in this age or in the age to come" (Matthew 12:31, 32).

Paul warned, "And do not grieve the Holy Spirit of God, by whom you were sealed for the day of redemption" (Ephesians 4:30).

Holy Ghost, the Infinite, shine upon our nature's night;
With Thy blessed, holy light, Comforter Divine.

We are sinful, cleanse us, Lord;
We are faint, Thy strength afford,
Lost, until by Thee restored, Comforter Divine.

In us, for us, intercede; and with voiceless groanings plead;
Our unutterable need, Comforter Divine.

In us "Abba, Father," cry, earnest of our bliss on high,
Seal of immortality, Comforter Divine.

—George Rawson

91

# God's Power on Our Behalf

*...That you may know what is the hope of His calling, what are the riches of the glory of His inheritance in the saints, and what is the exceeding greatness of His power toward us who believe, according to the working of His mighty power which He worked in Christ when He raised Him from the dead and seated Him at His right hand in the heavenly places...* (Ephesians 1:18b-20a).

This passage sums up the incredible blessings that accompany our redemption through Christ's blood. First of all, we have a hope, the promise of eternal life with Christ. Secondly, we are assured of God's power in our lives which is comparable to the power He exercised when He raised Christ from the dead! It requires as much power to give spiritual life to one who is spiritually dead, as it does to give physical life to one who is physically dead.

Paul wrote to the church in Colosse: "And you, being dead in your trespasses and the uncircumcision of your flesh, He has made alive together with Him [Christ], having forgiven you all trespasses...." (Colossians 2:13).

Paul went on to urge the Christians there: "If then you were raised with Christ, seek those things which are above, where Christ is sitting at the right hand of God" (Colossians 3:1).

Christ is risen! Hallelujah! Risen our victorious Head!
Sing His praises! Hallelujah! Christ is risen from the dead!
Gratefully our hearts adore Him,
As His light once more appears;
Bowing down in joy before Him, rising up from grief and tears.

Christ is risen! Henceforth never death or hell shall us enthrall;
We are Christ's, in Him forever we have triumphed over all;
All the doubting and dejection
Of our trembling hearts have ceased;
'Tis His day of resurrection! Rise and let us keep the feast!

—John B. Monsell

# God Raised Us with Christ

*But God, who is rich in mercy, because of His great love with which He loved us, even when we were dead in trespasses, made us alive together with Christ (by grace you have been saved) and raised us up together, and made us sit together in the heavenly places in Christ Jesus, that in the ages to come He might show the exceeding riches of His grace in His kindness toward us in Christ Jesus* (Ephesians 2:4-7)....

An unknown psalmist prophesied that the despised stone, rejected by the builders, would one day be proved to be the divinely-placed cornerstone of a new building (see Psalm 118:23). So God's people—now rejected as insignificant—will one day be honored with Christ, the "new cornerstone." And this is all by the grace of God. There is nothing we can do that deserves this distinction.

Before He went to the cross, Jesus promised His followers that He would return to "receive them to Himself," that they might be with Him forever (John 14:2, 3). He extended this promise to include us, who would believe on Him through their witness (John 17:20-24). Again, there is nothing we have done or can do to be worthy of such an honor; it is all of grace.

The stone rejected and despised is now the cornerstone;
How wondrous are the ways of God,
Unfathomed and unknown.

In this the day that Thou hast made, triumphantly we sing,
Send now prosperity, O Lord,
O Lord, salvation bring.

Hosanna! Ever blest be He that cometh in God's Name;
The blessing of Jehovah's house
Upon you we proclaim.

O Lord, my God, I praise Thy Name, all other names above;
O give Him thanks, for He is good
And boundless is His love.

—Psalter 318, Psalm 118

# Christ's Triumphant Ascension

*And* [God] *seated Him* [Christ] *at His right hand in the heavenly places, far above all principality and power and might and dominion, and every name that is named, not only in this age but also in that which is to come. And He put all things under His feet, and gave Him to be head over all things to the church, which is His body, the fullness of Him who fills all in all.* (Ephesians 1:18b-22).

While we receive new life with Christ's resurrection, we also receive a new destiny with His ascension. At His Father's right hand He reigns over all powers in the universe, not only in this age, but also in the age to come. He is the Head of the Church, which is now the "fullness of Him who fills all in all." Incredibly, the most insignificant of all believers will one day reign with Christ over all principalities and powers. We do not know all that this entails, but we rest on God's promise that it is all of grace.

"This was the Lord's doing; it is marvelous in our eyes" (Psalm 118:23).

> See the Conqueror mounts in triumph,
> See the King in royal state,
> Riding on the clouds His chariot to His heavenly palace gate;
> Hark! The choirs of angel voices joyful alleluias sing,
> And the portals high are lifted to receive their heavenly King.

> Who is this who comes in glory, with the trump of jubilee?
> Lord of battles, God of armies, He hath gained the victory.
> He who on the cross did suffer, He who from the grave arose,
> He has vanquished sin and Satan;
> He by death has spoiled His foes.

> Thou hast raised our human nature
> On the clouds to God's right hand;
> There we sit in heavenly places, there with Thee in glory stand.
> Jesus reigns, adored by angels, man with God is on the throne;
> Mighty Lord, in Thine ascension, we by faith behold our own.

—C. Wordsworth

# Saved by Grace

*For by grace you have been saved through faith, and that not of yourselves, it is the gift of God; not of works, lest anyone should boast. For we are His workmanship, created in Christ Jesus for good works, which God prepared beforehand that we should walk in them. ... Therefore remember that you were once Gentiles in the flesh—.... that you were at that time without Christ, being aliens from the commonwealth of Israel and strangers from the covenants of promise, having no hope and without God in the world. But now in Christ Jesus you who were once far off have been brought near by the blood of Christ* (Ephesians 2:8-11a, 12, 13).

Paul reminded his Gentile converts in Ephesus that their conversion to Christ was God's gift to them, and not the result of any effort on their behalf. As Gentiles, they had been cut off from the promises God made to the Israelites, but now, with Christ's death on the cross they had been admitted to "the commonwealth of Israel," and became sharers in the promises made to the Chosen People.

Dear friend, we who had no rights to or expectations of God's mercy, have been "accepted in the beloved", to the praise of His glory (Ephesians 1:6; 3:6)!

> Go to the deeps of God's promise;
> Ask freely of Him and receive;
> All good may be had for the asking,
> If seeking you truly believe.
>
> Go to the deeps of God's promise,
> And know of His wonderful might;
> Whatever would be a true blessing
> For Jesus' sake comes as your right.
>
> Go to the deeps of God's promise,
> The blessing is never denied;
> He loves, and remembers His children,
> And every good thing He supplies.

—Mrs. Frank A. Breck

# Groups United Through the Cross

*Now in Christ Jesus you who once were far off have been brought near by the blood of Christ. For He Himself is our peace, who has made both one, and has broken down the middle wall of separation, having abolished in His flesh the enmity, that is, the law of commandments contained in ordinances, so as to create in Himself one new man from the two, thus making peace, and that He might reconcile them both to God in one body through the cross....* (Ephesians 2:13-16a).

Through Christ's death on the cross, God has united people groups that historically were estranged linguistically, racially, by gender, and by distance. As the psalmists predicted (see verses below), all people groups will be united through Christ's reconciling death on the cross.

Currently, many divisions continue to exist between groups, but one day they will be unified, and all with one voice will praise the Lord of glory. "And every creature which is in heaven and on earth and under the earth, and all that are in them I heard, saying: 'Blessing and honor and glory and power be to Him, who sits on the throne, and to the Lamb, forever and ever'" (Revelation 5:13)!

> Our gracious God has laid His firm foundation
> On Zion's mount, the courts of His delight;
> Her gates of splendor, bathed in heavenly light,
> He loves far more than Jacob's habitation.
>
> What glorious things, O city of Jehovah,
> Are spoken in melodious tones of thee!
> Lo, Rahab, even Babel I will see,
> 'Mid hallowed chorus, singing Hallelujah.
>
> The Moor with the Philistine and the Tyrian
> Shall soon, O Zion, throng thy holy gate;
> In gladsome strains we'll hear her sons relate:
> "These all were born within the walls of Zion!"

—Psalter 442, Psalm 87

# The Essential Unity of the Church

*For through Him* [Jesus] *we have access by one Spirit to the Father. Now, therefore, you are no longer strangers and foreigners, but fellow-citizens with the saints and members of the household of God, having been built on the foundation of the apostles and prophets, Jesus Christ being the chief cornerstone in whom the whole building, being fitted together, grows into a holy temple of the Lord*...(Ephesians 2:18-20).

The apostle Paul explains the essential unity of the Church of Christ, which does not depend on us, but was made a reality when Christ died on the cross for all people groups. We are exhorted to "keep the unity of the Spirit in the bond of peace. There is one body and one Spirit, just as you were called in one hope of your calling: one Lord, one faith, one baptism, one God and Father of all" (Ephesians 4:3-6a)....

Dear friend, we must take care that our traditions do not rupture the unity of the body, but that we love our brothers and sisters in the faith with the same love wherewith Christ loved us when He laid down His life for the Church.

Maintaining the unity of the body is not easy. The apostle Paul lays down guidelines for handling debatable practices within the body in Romans 12:16; 14:1-23; and 1 Corinthians 10:23-33.

> Shout, for the blessed Jesus reigns,
> Through distant lands His triumph spreads;
> And sinners, freed from endless pains,
> Own Him their Savior and their Head.

> He calls His chosen from afar,
> They all at Zion's gates arrive,
> Those who were dead in sin before,
> By sovereign grace are made alive.

> Gentiles and Jews His laws obey,
> Nations remote their offerings bring,
> And unconstrained their homage pay
> To their exalted God and King.

—B. Beddome

# Paul Reveals the "Mystery of Christ"

*.... By the revelation He* [God] *made known to me* [Paul] *... the mystery of Christ, which in other ages was not made known to the sons of men ... that the Gentiles should be fellow heirs* [of the Jews], *of the same body, and partakers of His promise in Christ through the gospel....* (Ephesians 3:3-6).

The Ephesians were Gentiles who had been converted under Paul's ministry, but later were troubled by Jewish religious leaders who insisted they had to obey all the Old Testament laws in order to be saved. Paul explained that the "mystery of Christ" was that salvation is by grace for all, Jew and Gentile, since Christ had atoned for sin on the cross. He said, "For by grace you have been saved, through faith, and that not of yourselves, it is the gift of God; not of works, lest anyone should boast" (Ephesians 2:8, 9).

During the Old Testament era the Gentiles were welcomed into the temple worship on the basis of converting to the Jewish faith and submitting to all the laws that governed the lives of the Israelites. These Gentiles were called "God-fearers, or proselytes." Now, however, by decision of the apostles, the Gentiles were freely accepted into the Church on the basis of grace through faith, without being required to become proselytes (read Galatians 2:4-16).

> Free from the law, O happy condition,
> Jesus hath bled, and there is remission;
> Cursed by the law, and bruised by the Fall,
> Grace hath redeemed us, once for all.

> Now we are free, there's no condemnation,
> Jesus provides a perfect salvation;
> "Come unto Me," O hear His sweet call,
> Come, and He saves us once for all.

> "Children of God," O glorious calling,
> Surely His grace will keep us from falling;
> Passing from death to life at His call,
> Blessed salvation once for all.

> —P. P. Bliss

# Paul's Prayer for the Church

*For this reason I bow my knees to the Father of our Lord Jesus Christ from whom the whole family in heaven and earth is named, that He would grant you according to the riches of His glory to be strengthened with might through His Spirit in the inner man. That Christ may dwell in your hearts through faith, that you, being rooted and grounded in love, may be able to comprehend with all the saints what is the width and length and depth and height—to know the love of Christ which passes knowledge, that you may be filled with all the fullness of God* (Ephesians 3:14-19).

Paul prayed that we might experience the unknowable, and to be filled with the fullness of God who fills the universe. He wrote: "Who shall separate us from the love of Christ? Shall tribulation, or distress, or persecution, or famine, or nakedness, or peril, or sword? ... Yet in all these things we are more than conquerors through Him who loved us. For I am persuaded that neither death nor life, nor angels nor principalities nor powers, nor things present nor things to come, nor height nor depth, nor any other created thing shall be able to separate us from the love of God which is in Christ Jesus our Lord" (Romans 8:35-39).

It passeth knowledge, that dear love of Thine,
My Jesus, Savior, yet this soul of mine
Would of Thy love in all its breadth and length,
Its height and depth, its everlasting strength,
Know more and more.

It passeth telling, that dear love of Thine,
My Jesus, Savior, yet those lips of mine
Would fain proclaim to sinners far and near
A love which can remove all guilty fear
And love beget.

It passeth praises, that dear love of Thine,
My Jesus, Savior, yet this heart of mine
Would sing that love, so full, so rich, so free,
Which brings a rebel sinner, such as me,
Nigh unto God.

—Mary Shekleton

# Paul's Closing Prayer

*Now to Him who is able to do exceedingly abundantly above all that we ask or think, according to the power that works in us, to Him be glory in the church by Christ Jesus to all generations, forever and ever. Amen.*

*I, therefore, the prisoner of the Lord, beseech you to walk worthy of the calling with which you were called, with all lowliness and gentleness, with longsuffering, bearing with one another in love, endeavoring to keep the unity of the Spirit in the bond of peace....* (Ephesians 3:20, 21; 4:1-3).

The history of the Christian Church is scarred by conflict and divisions. Some discords are simply caused by geographical or linguistic distances, but others are the result of human ambition and pride. In His "high-priestly prayer" Jesus prayed for the unity of His followers: "... I come to You. Holy Father, keep through Your name those whom You have given Me, that they may be one as We are .... I do not pray for these alone, but also for those who will believe in Me through their word, that they all may be one, as You, Father, are in Me, and I in You, that they also may be one in Us, that the world may believe that You sent Me" (John 17:11b, 20, 21).

Father, I know that all my life is portioned out for me,
The changes that are sure to come, I do not fear to see;
I ask Thee for a present mind intent on pleasing Thee.

I ask Thee for a thoughtful love,
Through constant watching wise;
To meet the glad with joyful smiles,
To wipe the weeping eyes;
A heart at leisure from itself to soothe and sympathize.

In service which Thy will appoints there are no bonds for me;
My secret heart is taught the truth
That makes Thy children free:
A life of self-renouncing love is one of liberty.

—Anna L. Waring

# Sharing God's Love

*For He* [God] *chose us in Him* [Christ] *before the foundation of the world that we should be holy and without blame before Him in love, having predestined us to adoption as sons by Jesus Christ to Himself, according to the good pleasure of His will, to the praise of the glory of His grace, by which He made us accepted in the Beloved..... Therefore be imitators of God as dear children, and walk in love, as Christ also has loved us and given Himself for us, an offering and a sacrifice to God for a sweet-smelling aroma* (Ephesians 1:4-7; 5:1, 2).

In His "high-priestly" prayer, Jesus prayed that His followers might "be one, as You, Father, are in Me, and I in You, that they also may be one in Us, that the world may believe that You sent Me" (John 17:21). The mutual love between Christians is a powerful witness to the truth of the gospel and as long as we fail to love one another we provide Satan with convincing evidence that the gospel is neither true nor effective.

The apostle John argued, "He who does not love does not know God, for God is love... Beloved, if God so loved us, we also ought to love one another.... My little children, let us not love in word or in tongue, but in deed and in truth" (1 John 4:8, 11; 3:18).

How good and pleasant is the sight
When brethren make it their delight
To dwell in blest accord.
Such love is like anointing old
That consecrates for holy toil
The servants of the Lord.

Such love in peace and joy distills,
As o'er the slopes of Herman's hills
Refreshing dew descends;
The Lord commands His blessing there,
And they that walk in love shall share
In life that never ends.

—Psalter 370, Psalm 133

101

# God Completes His Work

*I thank my God upon every remembrance of you, always in every prayer of mine making request for you with joy, for your fellowship in the gospel from the first day and now. Being confident of this very thing, that He who has begun a good work in you will complete it unto the day of Jesus Christ* (Philippians 1:3-6).

In writing to the church at Philippi, Paul gave thanks to God for His faithfulness that we can depend on. Once God takes on a project, He carries it through to completion, never dropping it as "not worth the bother."

Paul wrote to the Corinthian church that God's promises can be trusted: "For all the promises of God in Him [Christ] are Yes, and in Him Amen, to the glory of God through us" (2 Corinthians 1:20).

Bemoaning the terrible fate of the city of Jerusalem and its populace, Jeremiah confessed that he would be desperate were it not for the mercies of God which never fail (Lamentations 3:20-24). He testified that "the Lord is good to those who wait for Him, to the soul who seeks Him."

Dear friend, amid the trials and disappointments you face, remember that God loves to be merciful, and that His everlasting arms are supporting you (Deuteronomy 33:27).

Cast thy burden on the Lord, only lean upon His Word,
Thou shalt soon have cause to bless
His unchanging faithfulness.

He sustains thee by His hand, He enables thee to stand;
Those whom Jesus once has loved,
From His grace are never moved.

Heaven and earth may pass away,
God's free grace will not decay.
He hath promised to fulfill all the pleasure of His will.

—Anonymous

# Paul Urges Unity in Suffering

*For to you it has been granted on behalf of Christ, not only to believe in Him, but also to suffer for His sake, having the same conflict which you saw in me and now hear is in me. Therefore if there is any consolation in Christ, if any comfort of love, if any fellowship of the Spirit, if any affection and mercy, fulfill my joy by being like-minded, having the same love, being of one accord, of one mind* (Philippians 1:29, 30; 2:1, 2).

It appears that there may have been serious problems of disagreements between members, because Paul repeats his exhortation in the final chapter of this epistle: "I implore Euodia and I implore Syntyche to be of the same mind in the Lord" (Philippians 4:2). In our fellowships such differences often occur, and we need to take Paul's recommendation to heart and not let our differing opinions cause rifts in the Christian community.

In His "sermon on the mount" Jesus warned His disciples to take care lest they exaggerate the importance of their differing opinions: "If your right eye causes you to sin, pluck it out and cast it from you; for it is more profitable for you that one of your members perish, than for your whole body to be cast into hell" (Matthew 5:29).

Our Father, Thou in heaven above,
Who biddest us to dwell in love,
As brethren of one family,
And cry for all we need to Thee;
Teach us to mean the words we say,
And from the inmost heart to pray.

Thy will be done on earth, O Lord,
As where in heaven Thou art adored!
Patience in time of grief bestow,
Obedience true in weal or woe;
Our sinful heart and will control,
That thwart Thy will within the soul.

—M. Luther, Tr. Miss C. Winkworth

# Christ: an Example of Humility

*Let this mind be in you which was also in Christ Jesus, who, being in the form of God, did not consider it robbery to be equal with God, but made Himself of no reputation, taking the form of a bondservant, and coming in the likeness of men. And being found in appearance as a man, He humbled Himself and became obedient to the point of death, even the death of the cross* (Philippians 2:5-8).

In urging the Philippian fellowship to cultivate a spirit of unity and love, the apostle Paul pointed out Christ's example. In an unprecedented act of humility, He took on our humanity and assumed the humble role of a poor itinerant preacher. His divine message provoked enough hostility on the part of the arrogant religious leaders that they sentence Him to die on a cross, with the most vile of criminals.

Because He was willing to submit to his role as the sacrificial Lamb, God has exalted Him above all other beings in the universe, so that He has decreed that to Jesus Christ "every knee shall bow and every tongue confess that Jesus Christ is Lord, to the glory of God the Father" (Philippians 2:9-11).

We must be careful to give Jesus Christ the honor that is due Him. He told the religious leaders: "The Father judges no one, but has committed all judgment to the Son, that all should honor the Son just as they honor the Father. He who does not honor the Son does not honor the Father who sent Him" (John 5:22, 23).

Majestic sweetness sits enthroned upon the Savior's brow;
His head with radiant glory crowned,
His lips with grace o'erflow.

No mortal can with Him compare among the sons of men;
Fairer is He than all the fair who fill the heavenly train.

He saw me plunged in deep despair and flew to my relief;
For me He bore the shameful cross, and carried all my grief.

To Him I owe my life and breath and all the joys I have;
He makes me triumph over death, and saves me from the grave.

—Anonymous

104

# God Works in His People

*Therefore, my beloved, as you have always obeyed,... work out your own salvation with fear and trembling, for it is God who works in you both to will and to do for His good pleasure. Do all things without complaining and disputing, that you may be blameless and harmless, children of God without fault....* (Philippians 2:12-15a).

Paul exhorted the Philippian Christians to dedicate themselves to a life of obedience to God, reminding them that ultimately the work is the Lord's, and not ours, and that God takes pleasure in conforming us to the image of His Son. In this Paul echoes David's prayer in Psalm 138 (below), assured that God will never abandon a work He has begun. David was confident that God would "revive and strengthen" him in his hour of need.

Dear friend, when our health fails, we become discouraged, feeling that God has abandoned us. But God is not subject to moods, as we are. His purposes are established from eternity. Paul reminded the Philippians: "For our citizenship is in heaven, from which we also eagerly wait for the Savior, the Lord Jesus Christ, who will transform our lowly body that it may be conformed to His glorious body according to the working by which He is able even to subdue all things to Himself" (Philippians 3:20, 21).

> O Lord, enthroned in glory bright,
> Thou reignest in the heavenly heights.
> The proud in vain Thy favor seek,
> But Thou hast mercy for the meek;
> Through trouble though my pathway be,
> Thou wilt revive and strengthen me.
>
> Thou wilt stretch forth Thy mighty arm
> To save me when my foes alarm;
> The work Thou hast in me begun,
> Shall by Thy grace be fully done.
> Forever mercy dwells with Thee;
> O Lord, my Maker, think on me.

> Psalter 381, Psalm 138

# Paul's Reminder to Rejoice

*Rejoice in the Lord always. Again I will say, rejoice! Let your gentleness be known to all men. The Lord is at hand.*

*Be anxious for nothing, but in everything by prayer and supplication, with thanksgiving, let your requests be made known to God; and the peace of God, which surpasses all understanding, will guard your hearts and minds through Christ Jesus* (Philippians 4:4-7).

Paul's exhortation reminds us of Isaiah's prescription for peace of mind. He prayed: "You will keep him in perfect peace, whose mind is stayed on You, because he trusts in You. Trust in the LORD forever, for in YAH, the LORD, is everlasting strength" (Isaiah 26:3, 4).

As Paul faced his final days on earth, he reminded the Church of the power of praise and of joy in the Lord. We remember that Nehemiah exhorted the repentant returnees from exile that the time had come to rejoice in the Lord for His grace and forgiveness. He said, "Do not sorrow, for the joy of the LORD is your strength." (Nehemiah 8:10b).

An unknown psalmist sang:

> O praise ye the Lord and sing a new song,
> Amid all His saints His praises prolong;
> The praise of their Maker His people shall sing,
> And children of Zion rejoice in their King.

> With timbrel and harp and joyful acclaim,
> With gladness and mirth sing praise to His Name.
> For God in His people His pleasure doth seek,
> With robes of salvation He clotheth the meek.

> For this is His word, His saints shall not fail,
> But over the earth their power shall prevail;
> All kingdoms and nations shall yield to their sway,
> To God be the glory and praise Him for aye.

—Psalter 407, Psalm 149

106

# Paul's Testimony

[Paul testified:] *I know how to be abased, and I know how to abound. Everywhere and in all things I have learned both to be full and to be hungry, both to abound and to suffer need. I can do all things through Christ who strengthens me…. And my God shall supply all your need according to His riches in glory by Christ Jesus* (Philippians 4:12, 13, 19).

David sang that his heavenly Shepherd had pledged Himself to provide for all his needs: "The LORD is my Shepherd; I shall not want" (Psalm 23:1). The apostle Paul concurred at the end of a turbulent life of ministry that he "could do all things through Christ," and that the Philippian Christians could expect the same care from the Lord.

Dear friend, this does not mean that God has promised to provide all we could wish for, but that He will take care of all we need because He is an infinitely rich God who has become our heavenly Father when He adopted us in Christ.

All the way my Savior leads me, what have I to ask beside?
Can I doubt His tender mercy,
Who through life has been my guide?
Heavenly peace, divinest comfort,
Here by faith in Him to dwell.
For I know, whate'er befalls me, Jesus doeth all things well.

All the way my Savior leads me,
Cheers each winding path I tread,
Gives me grace for every trial, feeds me with the living bread.
Though my weary steps may falter,
And my soul athirst may be,
Gushing from the Rock before me, lo! a spring of joy I see.

All the way my Savior leads me. Oh, the fullness of His love!
Perfect rest to me is promised in my Father's house above.
When my spirit, meet for glory,
Wings its flight to realms of day,
This my song through endless ages: Jesus led me all the way.

—Fanny J. Crosby

# Paul Unveils God's Mystery

*To them* [the saints] *God willed to make known what are the riches of the glory of the mystery among the Gentiles: which is Christ in you, the hope of glory. Him we preach, warning every man and teaching every man in all wisdom, that we may present every man perfect in Christ Jesus* (Colossians 1:27, 28).

The Judaizers firmly believed that the only hope the Gentiles had of salvation was by submitting to all the Jewish laws. Paul reminded the Colossians that, on the contrary, the only hope of salvation was to be found in Jesus Christ, whether one was a Jew or a Gentile. It is Christ in the believer that guarantees his hope of eternal salvation.

Paul insisted that no works of any kind can qualify a sinner for eternal life. He wrote to the Ephesians: "For by grace you have been saved through faith, and that not of yourselves; it is the gift of God, not of works, lest anyone should boast" (Ephesians 2:8-10).

The Jewish apostle explained to the Galatians, "I have been crucified with Christ; it is no longer I who live, but Christ lives in me; and the life which I now live in the flesh I live by faith in the Son of God, who loved me and gave Himself for me" (Galatians 2:20).

My only hope must be in Jesus,
Who made atonement for my sin;
There is no other power to help me,
Alone in Christ I must begin.

My only hope must be in Jesus,
No other Friend of love divine;
No other sacrifice beside Him,
Who made such great salvation mine.

There is no other Savior given,
No other hope beyond the grave,
No other Name in earth or heaven,
My guilty, dying soul to save.

—Ina Duley Ogdon

# The New Life in Christ

*You, being dead in your trespasses and the uncircumcision of your flesh, He has made alive together with Him, having forgiven you all trespasses,... He has taken it out of the way, having nailed it to the cross.... If you then were raised with Christ, seek those things which are above, where Christ is sitting at the right hand of God. ...For you died, and your life is hidden with Christ in God* (Colossians 2:13, 14; 3:1, 3).

Paul reminded the believers in Colosse that they were now new people, because God raised them from spiritual death when He raised Christ from the grave. Because they were new people, they needed to project a new image: that of people made alive through Christ's resurrection.

What a wonderful picture we have here of salvation! When God raised Christ from the grave He also gave us—sinners who were "dead in trespasses and sins"—new life in His Son. When Jesus died our sins were buried with Him. When He died, our old life died, says Paul, and when He arose, we received new spiritual life. This new life should identify with Jesus Christ, leading us to be more like our Savior.

Dying with Jesus, by death reckoned mine;
Living with Jesus, a new life divine;
Looking to Jesus till glory doth shine,
Moment by moment, O Lord, I am Thine.

Never a trial that He is not there,
Never a burden that He doth not bear,
Never a sorrow that He doth not share,
Moment by moment, I'm under His care.

Never a weakness that He doth not feel,
Never a sickness that He cannot heal;
Moment by moment, in woe or in weal,
Jesus, my Savoir, abides with me still.

—D. H. Whittle

# Characteristics of the New Life

*Therefore, as the elect of God, holy and beloved, put on tender mercies, kindness, humility, meekness, longsuffering; bearing with one another, and forgiving one another, if anyone has a complaint against another; even as Christ forgave you, so you also must do. But above all these things put on love, which is the bond of perfection. And let the peace of God rule in your hearts* (Colossians 3:12-14).

It is hard to stifle our selfish impulses and to put our brother's interest before our own! Also, to be a follower of Jesus Christ means that we must put our heavenly Father's interests before our own, just as Jesus did, when He willingly went to the cross because it was His Father's will.

Jesus' words to His disciples in the final hours of His earthly ministry highlight the importance of Christian love: "By this all will know that you are My disciples, if you have love for one another" (John 13:35).

The apostle John wrote: "Beloved, let us love one another, for love is of God and everyone who loves is born of God and knows God. He who does not love does not know God, for God is love" (1 John 4:7, 8).

> How sweet, how heavenly is the sight,
> When those that love the Lord,
> In one another's peace delight,
> And thus fulfill His word.
>
> When free from envy, scorn and pride,
> Our wishes all above,
> Each can his brother's failings hide,
> And show a brother's love.
>
> Love is a golden chain that binds
> The happy souls above,
> And he's an heir of heaven who finds
> His bosom glow with love.

—Joseph Swain

# Serve Others for Christ's Sake

*Whatever you do, do it heartily as to the Lord and not to men, knowing that from the Lord you will receive the reward of the inheritance, for you serve the Lord Christ.... Let your speech always be with grace, seasoned with salt, that you may know how you ought to answer each one* (Colossians 3:17; 4:7).

Paul's advice to the Colossians is very challenging. How can our speech be "seasoned with salt"? It probably doesn't mean what we speak of as "salty speech," but surely it means making the truth of what we say as acceptable as possible to the hearer. Certainly the exhortation to let our speech always be with grace implies this.

When the Lord Jesus rebuked the hypocrisy of the scribes and Pharisees He did not mince words. He called a spade a spade. Yet He remained accessible to those who sought Him out for counsel (such as Nicodemus, in John 3), and verses 16 and 17 of that chapter show His grace to a sincere seeker.

Surely we need God's wisdom to discern "how we ought to answer" each person who challenges us!

Fill Thou my life, O Lord, my God in every part with praise,
That my whole being may proclaim Thy being and Thy ways;
Not for the lip of praise alone, nor e'en the praising heart,
I ask, but for a life made up of praise in every part.

Praise in the common words I speak,
Life's common looks and tones,
In intercourse at hearth or board with my beloved ones—
Enduring wrong, reproach, or loss with sweet and steadfast will,
Loving and blessing those who hate, returning good for ill.

So shall each fear, each fret, each care be turned into a song
And every winding of the way the echo shall prolong;
So shall no part of day or night from sacredness be free,
But all my life, in every step be fellowship with Thee.

—Horatius Bonar

# The Holy Spirit is our Guarantee

*Now He who establishes us with you in Christ and has anointed us is God, who has also sealed us and given us the Spirit in our hearts as a guarantee* (2 Corinthians 1:21, 22).

The apostle Paul assured the Corinthians that the gift of the Holy Spirit in our hearts is God's guarantee that we will receive a complete salvation and all that it involves, in due time. What a comfort to know that we will eventually be redeemed from even the tendency to sin and be made like Jesus Christ. The apostle John wrote: "Behold, now we are children of God, and it has not yet been revealed what we shall be, but we know that when He is revealed, we shall be like Him, for we shall see Him as He is" (1 John 3:2)!

The apostle Paul wrote: "As many as are led by the Spirit of God, these are sons of God. For you did not receive the spirit of bondage again to fear, but you received the Spirit of adoption, by whom we cry out, 'Abba, Father.' The Spirit Himself bears witness with our spirit that we are children of God, and if children, then heirs—heirs of God and joint heirs with Christ...." (Romans 8:14-17a).

Dwell in me, O blessed Spirit,
How I need Thy help divine!
In the way of life eternal,
Keep, O keep this heart of mine!

Round the cross where Thou hast led me,
Let my purest feelings twine;
With the blood from sin that cleansed me,
Seal anew this heart of mine.

Dwell in me, O blessed Spirit,
Gracious Teacher, Friend divine,
For the home of bliss that waits me,
O prepare this heart of mine.

—Martha J. Lankton

# We Are the Fragrance of Christ

*Now thanks be to God who always leads us in triumph in Christ and through us diffuses the fragrance of His knowledge in every place. For we are to God the fragrance of Christ among those who are being saved and among those who are perishing. To the one we are the aroma of death tending to death, and to the other the aroma of life leading to life* (2 Corinthians 2:14-16a).

The apostle Paul reminded the Corinthian believers that they were representing the Lord Jesus Christ to the world. This means that to His enemies the Christians exuded the odor of death, so they hated them, but to those who were open to the work of the Spirit, they radiated a life-giving aroma that attracted them.

We all want to be loved and appreciated, but if Jesus—who was the only sinless human being who ever existed—was hated, who only went about doing good, we should not be amazed if we encounter people who hate us because we are Christians. Jesus told His disciples: "If the world hates you, you know that it hated Me before it hated you. If you were of the world, the world would love its own. Yet because you are not of the world, but I chose you out of the world, therefore the world hates you" (John 15:18, 19).

> More about Jesus would I know,
> More of His grace to others show;
> More of His saving fullness see,
> More of His love who died for me.
>
> More about Jesus let me learn,
> More of His holy will discern;
> Spirit of God, my teacher be,
> Showing the things of Christ to me.
>
> More about Jesus in His Word,
> Holding communion with my Lord,
> Hearing His voice in every line,
> Making each faithful saying mine.

—E. E. Hewitt

# A Transformation in Process

*But we all, with unveiled face, beholding as in a mirror the glory of the Lord, are being transformed into the same image from glory to glory, just as by the Spirit of the Lord.... For it is God who commanded light to shine out of darkness, who has shone in our hearts to give the light of the knowledge of the glory of God in the face of Jesus Christ. But we have this treasure in earthen vessels, that the excellence of the power may be of God and not of us* (2 Corinthians 3:18; 4:6, 7).

The apostle Paul pointed out that the transformation of the repentant sinner into a saint who bears the image of the Savior is the work of the triune God. He has "shone in our hearts to give the light of the knowledge of the glory of God in the face of Jesus Christ." This is a divine work in our hearts, and not something that we can attain by concerted efforts.

Some years ago I remember seeing an occasional person wearing a pin on which was inscribed, "I am a work in process." This continues to be true in the Christian life. We are reminded of Paul's words to the Philippians: "...Work out your own salvation with fear and trembling; for it is God who works in you both to will and to do for His good pleasure" (Philippians 2:12b, 13).

O to be like Thee! Blessed Redeemer,
This is my constant longing and prayer;
Gladly I'll forfeit all of earth's treasures,
Jesus, Thy perfect likeness to wear!

O to be like Thee! Full of compassion,
Loving, forgiving, tender and kind;
Helping the helpless, cheering the fainting,
Seeking the wandering sinner to find.

O to be like Thee! While I am pleading,
Pour out Thy Spirit, fill with Thy love;
Make me a temple meet for Thy dwelling,
Fit me for life and heaven above.

—Thomas O. Chisholm

# Seeing the Unseen

*Therefore we do not lose heart. Even though our outward man is perishing, yet the inward man is being renewed day by day. For our light affliction, which is but for a moment, is working for us a far more exceeding and eternal weight of glory, while we do not look at the things which are seen, but at the things which are not seen, for the things which are seen are temporary, but the things which are not seen are eternal* (2 Corinthians 4:16-18).

The apostle Paul called the attention of the church at Corinth to the only truly lasting values in this life. As his life was drawing to a close, and he waited for his death sentence to be implemented, he reminded the suffering church that the only lasting values were the invisible ones. He refers to them as the "far more exceeding and eternal weight of glory," and urges the Corinthians and us to keep our attention focused on these.

As our "outward man is perishing," we need to remind ourselves of the "more exceeding and eternal weight of glory" which surpasses all earthy values. It is by sovereign grace that our feet have been planted on the Rock of Ages.

> We would see Jesus, for the shadows lengthen
> Across the little landscape of our life;
> We would see Jesus, our weak faith to strengthen,
> For the last weariness, the final strife.
>
> We would see Jesus, the great rock foundation
> Whereon our feet were set by sovereign grace;
> Not life nor death, with all their agitation,
> Can thence remove us, if we see His face.
>
> We would see Jesus—other lights are paling,
> Which for long years we have rejoiced to see;
> The blessings of our pilgrimage are failing:
> We would not mourn them, for we go to Thee.
>
> We would see Jesus—this is all we're needing, ...
> Then, welcome day! and farewell, mortal night!
>
> —Anna B. Warner

# A Purpose-Driven Life

*For the love of Christ compels us, because we judge thus: that if One died for all, then all died; and He died for all, that those who live should no longer live for themselves, but for Him who died for them and rose again. ... Therefore, if anyone is in Christ, he is a new creation; old things have passed away; behold, all things have become new* (2 Corinthians 5:14, 15, 17).

Paul's message recalls God's promise to the dispersed people of Judah: "This is what the Sovereign LORD says: I will gather you from the nations and bring you back from the countries where you have been scattered, and I will give you back the land of Israel again. They will return to it and remove all the vile images and detestable idols. I will give them an undivided heart and put a new spirit in them. I will remove from them their heart of stone and give them a heart of flesh. Then they will follow my decrees and be careful to keep my laws. They will be my people, and I will be their God" (Ezekiel 11:17-20).

We know that in the New Testament era there was no sign of idol worship among the Jews any more, but Paul was writing about a new life in Christ for those who turned to Him in repentance. When Christ died on the cross, we, who believe on Him, died with Him. We were raised to new life with His resurrection. Thus our lives now belong to Him, for He took on Himself the penalty for our sins that we might be eternally free from their guilt.

> O for a heart to praise my God, a heart from sin set free;
> A heart that's sprinkled with the blood
> So freely shed for me!

> A heart in every thought renewed, and full of love divine,
> Perfect and right, and pure and good,
> A copy, Lord, of Thine.

> Thy nature, gracious Lord, impart; come quickly from above;
> Write Thy new name upon my heart,
> Thy new, best name, of love.

—Charles Wesley

# Avoid an Unequal Yoke

*Do not be unequally yoked together with unbelievers. For what fellowship has righteousness with lawlessness? And what communion has light with darkness? And what accord has Christ with Belial? Or what part has a believer with an unbeliever? And what agreement has the temple of God with idols? For you are the temple of the living God* (2 Corinthians 6:14-16a).

It appears that Paul is here forbidding any close cooperation between the false teachers and the Corinthian Christians. These verses have often been used to discourage intermarriage between a Christian and an unbeliever. Perhaps a "mixed" business partnership between believer and unbeliever may also be implied. The call to holiness is a call to separation from what is evil so that the believer may serve God with undivided heart.

In societies where marriages are arranged by clan leaders or family heads, the individuals involved have little or no voice in the choice of a spouse. In our modern societies, however, the individuals do have options, and should be aware that partnership with an unbeliever is often a strong negative influence in a Christian's life.

May the mind of Christ my Savior
Live in me from day to day,
By His love and power controlling all I do and say.

May the Word of God dwell richly
In my heart from hour to hour;
So that all may see I conquer only by His power.

May the love of Jesus fill me
As the waters fill the sea;
Him exalting, self abasing—this is victory.

May I run the race before me,
Strong and brave to face the foe;
Looking only unto Jesus as I onward go.

—Kate B. Wilkinson

# Christ, an Example of Generosity

*For you know the grace of our Lord Jesus Christ, that though He was rich, yet for your sakes He became poor, that you through His poverty might become rich…. For if there is first a willing mind, it is accepted according to what one has, and not according to what he does not have* (2 Corinthians 8:9, 12).

As Paul exhorted the Corinthians to be liberal in their giving, he pointed to the Savior as an example. Christ was willing to give up every advantage as Creator and Sovereign of the universe so that He could redeem fallen mankind that had thrown away its high position as God's most privileged creature only to taste the forbidden fruit.

Christ, the eternal Son of God, was born in a stable, raised in a carpenter's poor home in Nazareth, a deprived village. When He reached adulthood, he traveled as an itinerant evangelist and healer, and finally died on a cruel cross between two criminals. The writer to the Hebrews described His willingness to give up everything: "Who for the joy that was set before Him, endured the cross, despising the shame…" (Hebrews 12:2).

My life, my love, I give to Thee,
Thou Lamb of God, who died for me;
O may I ever faithful be,
My Savior and my God.

I now believe, Thou dost receive,
For Thou hast died that I might live;
And now henceforth I'll trust in Thee,
My Savior and my God.

O Thou who died on Calvary,
To save my soul and make me free,
I'll consecrate my life to Thee,
My Savior and my God.

—Ralph E. Hudson

# God Rewards the Generous Giver

[Paul wrote:] *But this I say: He who sows sparingly will also reap sparingly, and he who sows bountifully will also reap bountifully. So let each one give as he purposes in his heart, not grudgingly or of necessity, for God loves a cheerful giver. And God is able to make all grace abound toward you, that you, always having all sufficiency in all things, may have an abundance for every good work* (2 Corinthians 9:6-8).

In his letter to the church of Galatia, Paul wrote that the kinds of seeds we sow will determine what our harvest will be: "Do not be deceived, God is not mocked; for whatever a man sows, that he will also reap. For he who sows to his flesh will of the flesh reap corruption, but he who sows to the Spirit will of the Spirit reap everlasting life" (Galatians 6:7, 8). Here to the Corinthians he says that our attitudes toward giving will determine how large the rewards will be. The reluctant giver will have a scanty harvest, while God will bless the liberal giver.

The blessings are promised for the giver who rejoices in giving, not necessarily to the one who can give the larger amount.

> More about Jesus would I know,
> More of His grace to others show,
> More of His saving fullness see,
> More of His love, who died for me.
>
> More about Jesus let me learn,
> More of His holy will discern,
> Spirit of God, my teacher be,
> Showing the things of Christ to me.
>
> More about Jesus in His Word,
> Holding communion with my Lord,
> Hearing His voice in every line,
> Making each faithful saying mine.

—Eliza E. Hewitt

# Paul's Confession

[Paul wrote:] *Concerning this thing* [his "thorn in the flesh"] *I pleaded with the Lord three times that it might depart from me. And He said to me, "My grace is sufficient for you, for My strength is made perfect in weakness." Therefore most gladly I will rather boast in my infirmities, that the power of Christ may rest upon me. Therefore I take pleasure in infirmities, in reproaches, in needs, in persecutions, in distresses, for Christ's sake. For when I am weak, then I am strong"* (2 Corinthians 12:8-10).

There has been much debate as to the nature of Paul's "thorn in the flesh," but it seems to have been some kind of physical handicap, perhaps even an embarrassing pathological condition. Whatever it was, Paul earnestly prayed for God to remove it, but God said, "No." His grace is sufficient to overcome all of our handicaps, and God is glorified in the consecrated lives of His handicapped servants.

The amazing sequel to this episode is that Paul bowed under God's decision, and even "took pleasure" in suffering from this "thorn" so that God might have all the glory for Paul's ministry.

Dear friend, let us bow under God's providence and accept what He sends us, knowing that our heavenly Father's way is the best way.

> God's way is the best way, though I may not see
> Why sorrows and trials oft gather round me;
> He ever is seeking my gold to refine,
> So humbly I'll trust Him, my Savior divine.
>
> God's way is the best way, my path He hath planned;
> I'll trust in Him always while holding His hand.
> In shadow or sunshine, He ever is near,
> With Him as my refuge, I never need fear.
>
> God's way is the best way, God's way is the right way.
> I'll trust in Him alway, He knoweth the best.

> —Lida Shivers Leech

# The Faithful Thessalonians

*From you the word of the Lord has sounded forth, not only in Macedonia and Achaia, but also in every place. Your faith toward God has gone out, so that we do not need to say anything. For they themselves declare concerning us what manner of entry we had to you, and how you turned to God from idols to serve the living and true God, and to wait for His Son from heaven, whom He raised from the dead, even Jesus, who delivers us from the wrath to come* (1 Thessalonians 1:8-10).

Paul was accustomed to begin each of his epistles with a word of commendation and encouragement. Apparently the report had traveled widely about the radical change in the lives of the Christians in Thessalonica, and Paul rejoiced to hear the encouraging news.

The new believers in Thessalonica not only turned from idols to worshiping the true God, but they were eagerly looking forward to Christ's second coming. My husband and I were delighted when José Leão (a Brazilian Indian from the Maxakalí tribe) told us that he looked toward the sky both morning and evening, watching for Christ's return. He complained to Harold, "Why doesn't He come?" I was ashamed to admit that I seldom dared to hope that He would come that day.

Dear friend, let us not neglect to anticipate that glorious day when Christ will return in triumph to gather His Church from the "four corners of the earth."

> When Jesus comes to reward His servants,
> Whether it be noon or night,
> Faithful to Him will He find us watching,
> With our lamps all trimmed and bright?
>
> Blessed are those whom the Lord finds watching,
> In His glory they shall share;
> If He shall come at the dawn or midnight,
> Will He find us watching there?
>
> —Fanny J. Crosby

# The Dead Will Rise First....

*...We who are alive and remain until the coming of the Lord will by no means precede those who are asleep. For the Lord Himself will descend from heaven with a shout, with the voice of an archangel, and with the trumpet of God, and the dead in Christ will rise first. Then we who are alive and remain shall be caught up together with them in the clouds to meet the Lord in the air. And thus we shall always be with the Lord. Therefore comfort one another with these words* (1 Thessalonians 4:15b-18).

To comfort the Thessalonian believers who feared that the believers who had died might miss the glorious event of Christ's return, Paul assured them that the dead believers will have precedence over those living when Christ returns in triumph.

After some two thousand years it is not as easy to believe that Christ's return is imminent. I remember in the 1970s that many songs were being composed to celebrate Christ's return, believed to be imminent. When Jesus said that He was "coming quickly" (Revelation 22:20), the early Church believed that it would be any day. Yet Jesus warned His followers that we must be ready: "Watch, therefore, for you know neither the day nor the hour in which the Son of Man is coming" (Matthew 25:13).

Soon will our Savior from heaven appear.
Sweet is the hope and its power to cheer;
All will be changed by a glimpse of His face—
This is the goal at the end of our race!

Loneliness changed to reunion complete,
Absence exchanged for a place at His feet.
Sleeping ones raised in a moment of time,
Living ones changed to His image sublime!

Oh, what a change!
When I shall see His face!

—Ada R. Habershon

# The Lord Will Return without Warning

[Paul wrote:] *For you yourselves know perfectly that the day of the Lord will come as a thief in the night..... But you, brethren, are not in darkness, so that this Day should overtake you as a thief. You are all sons of light and sons of the day....*

*Therefore let us not sleep, as others do, but let us watch and be sober, putting on the breastplate of faith and love, and as a helmet, the hope of salvation. For God did not appoint us to wrath, but to obtain salvation through our Lord Jesus Christ* (1 Thessalonians 4:6, 8, 9).

Although there will be no obvious warning that the time of Christ's return is at hand, He does require that we be ready. He illustrated this requirement by presenting the Jews with several parables, in which the rewards of readiness and the penalties of a failure to prepare were clearly shown. Here Paul reminds the Thessalonians that they are "sons of light," and there was no excuse for not being ready for Christ's return.

> Sooner or later, the skies will be bright,
> Tears will be all wiped away;
> Sooner or later, there cometh the light,
> Night will be turned into day.

> Sooner or later, our Lord knows the hour,
> He'll send His beloved Son;
> Sooner or later, in His might and power,
> Our battles all will be won.

> Sooner or later, sooner for some,
> Darkness will all then be past;
> Sooner or later, our Savior will come,
> With Him will your lot be cast?...

> Sooner or later God calleth His own,
> With Him forever to be.

> — Lula W. Koch

# The Revelation of the "Man of Sin"

*Let no one deceive you by any means, for that Day* [of Christ's return] *will not come unless the falling away comes first, and the man of sin is revealed, the son of perdition, who opposes and exalts himself above all that is called God or that is worshiped, so that he sits as God in the temple of God, showing himself that he is God* (2 Thessalonians 2:3, 4).

The Thessalonians had been troubled by rumors that Christ had already returned, and they had been left behind. Paul reassured them that it was not true. He reminded them: "Do you not remember that when I was still with you I told you these things? And now you know what is restraining, that he may be revealed in his own time" (2 Thessalonians 2:5, 6).

What Paul called the "man of sin," the apostle John called the "Antichrist" (1 John 4:3-5). He goes into great detail about his persecution of the saints in his prophetic book of Revelation (the last book of the Bible). He also shows the Antichrist's final torment in the Lake of Fire, after he is condemned by Christ in the final judgment (Revelation 19:19-20:10).

> Oft times the day seems long, our trials hard to bear,
> We're tempted to complain, to murmur and despair;
> But Christ will soon appear and catch His bride away.
> All tears forever over in God's eternal day.
>
> Sometimes the sky looks dark with not a ray of light,
> We're tossed and driven on, no human help in sight;
> But there is one in heaven who knows our deepest care,
> Let Jesus solve your problem—just go to Him in prayer.
>
> Life's day will soon be o'er, all storms forever past.
> We'll cross the great divide, to glory, safe at last;
> We'll share the joys of heaven, a harp, a home, a crown,
> The tempter will be banished, we'll lay our burdens down.
>
> It will be worth it all, when we see Jesus!
> Our trials will seem so small when we see Christ! …
>
> —Esther Kerr Rusthoi

# Lifestyle Commands

*For you yourselves know how you ought to follow us, for we were not disorderly among you, nor did we eat anyone's bread free of charge.... For even when we were with you, we commanded you thus: If anyone will not work, neither shall he eat* (2 Thessalonians 3:7, 8, 10).

The assembly of Thessalonian believers was troubled by a number of members who did not work at all, but expected to be supported by others. They became a burden to the fellowship, and Paul had laid down the rule while he was with them, that those who refused to work should not be fed by those who were laboring to support themselves and their families. Apparently they had reverted to their idle behavior during Paul's absence, so he reminded the church that they were not to feed the lazy members who were unwilling to work.

When God created Adam, He "put him in the Garden of Eden to tend and keep it" (Genesis 2:15). Work is a basic function of God's human creatures and not merely a curse imposed on humanity after the Fall.

> Day by day, and with each passing moment
> Strength I find to meet my trials here;
> Trusting in my Father's wise bestowment,
> I've no cause for worry or for fear.
>
> He whose heart is kind beyond all measure
> Gives unto each day what He deems best—
> Lovingly, its part of pain and pleasure,
> Mingling toil with peace and rest.
>
> Help me, Lord, when toil and trouble meeting,
> E'er to take, as from a father's hand,
> One by one, the days, the moments fleeting,
> Till I reach the promised land.
>
> —Lina Sandell Berg, trans. Andrew L. Skoog

# Respect Your Leaders

*We urge you, brethren, to recognize those who labor among you, and are over you in the Lord and admonish you, and esteem them very highly in love for their work's sake. Be at peace among yourselves* (1 Thessalonians 5:12, 13).

We appreciate our leaders when they applaud our efforts, but when they perceive that we are slacking off, and have the nerve to tell us about their perception, we resent them. Paul told the Thessalonians that they need to recognize that these leaders—who had sufficient courage to critique their faults—are to be "esteemed very highly" for their loving care, and they should not be resentful of their frankness.

When the prophet Hanani came to King Asa with God's message, rebuking the king for calling on the king of Syria rather than on the Lord, Asa was so infuriated that he threw the prophet in prison, and refused to invoke God's blessing even when he was stricken with a fatal disease of his feet (2 Chronicles 16:7-12).

How different was King Nebuchadnezzar's response to Daniel's interpretation of his dream! Although he did not repent, he did not punish Daniel for his shocking prophesy (Daniel 4:27).

> Trying to walk in the steps of the Savior,
> Trying to follow our Savior and King;
> Shaping our lives by His blessed example,
> Happy, how happy the praises we sing.
>
> Pressing more closely to Him who is leading,
> When we are tempted to turn from the way;
> Trusting the arm that is strong to defend us,
> Happy, how happy our praises each day.
>
> Walking in footsteps of gentle forbearance,
> Footsteps of faithfulness, mercy, and love;
> Looking to Him for His grace freely promised,
> Happy, how happy our journey above.

—E. E. Hewitt

# Exhortation Summary

*Now we exhort you, brethren, warn those who are unruly, comfort the fainthearted, uphold the weak, be patient with all. See that no one renders evil for evil to anyone, but always pursue what is good both for yourselves and for all. Rejoice always. Pray without ceasing. In everything give thanks, for this is the will of God in Christ Jesus for you* (1 Thessalonians 5:14-18).

In the verses above, Paul pointed out what is God's will for our Christian lives. Seeing that beautiful summary of what our Christian lives should look like, we must admit that few of us can spread the fragrance of Christ's love to the world in the manner described by those verses.

Paul wrote: "We are to God the fragrance of Christ among those who are being saved and among those who are perishing. To the one we are the aroma of death leading to death, and to the other the aroma of life leading to life" (2 Corinthians 2:15, 16). In a message of encouragement, he wrote: "But we all, with unveiled face, beholding as in a mirror the glory of the Lord, are being transformed into the same image from glory to glory, just as by the Spirit of the Lord" (2 Corinthians 3:18).

I am not worthy, holy Lord,
That Thou shouldst come to me,
Speak but the word, one gracious word
Can set the sinner free.

I am not worthy, cold and bare
The lodging of my soul;
How canst Thou deign to enter there?
Lord, speak and make me whole.

O come! In this sweet sacred hour,
Feed me with food divine;
And fill with all Thy love and power
This worthless heart of mine.

—Henry W. Baker

# Our Sole Mediator

*Who* [God] *desires all men to be saved and to come to the knowledge of the truth. For there is one God and one Mediator between God and men, the Man Christ Jesus, who gave Himself a ransom for all to be testified in due time….* (1 Timothy 2:4-6).

Paul was emphatic in stating that there is only one mediator between God and men: our Lord Jesus Christ. Earlier, the apostles Peter and John had affirmed to the Jewish Sanhedrin that only Jesus qualified as Savior: "Nor is there salvation in any other, for there is no other name under heaven given among men by which we must be saved" (Acts 4:12).

The apostle John further affirmed: "My little children, these things I write to you, so that you may not sin. And if anyone sins, we have an Advocate with the Father, Jesus Christ the righteous. And He is the propitiation for our sins, and not for ours only but also for the whole world" (1 John 2:1, 2).

The unknown author of the book of Hebrews wrote: "He [Jesus] is also able to save to the uttermost those who come to God through Him, since He always lives to make intercession for them" (Hebrews 8:25).

Hail, Thou once despised Jesus;
Hail, Thou Galilean King!
Thou didst suffer to release us,
Thou didst free salvation bring.
Hail, Thou agonizing Savior, bearer of our sin and shame!
By Thy merits we find favor, life is given through Thy Name.

Paschal Lamb, by God appointed,
All our sins on Thee were laid.
By almighty love anointed,
Thou hast full atonement made.
All Thy people are forgiven, through the virtue of Thy blood;
Opened is the gate to heaven,
Peace is made 'twixt man and God.

—John Bakewell

# Jesus Is Affirmed as God

*Without controversy, great is the mystery of godliness: "God was manifested in the flesh, justified in the Spirit, seen by angels, preached among the Gentiles, believed on in the world, received up in glory"* (1 Timothy 3:16).

[Jesus said to Thomas:] *"Reach your finger here, and look at My hands; and reach your hand here, and put it into My side. Do not be unbelieving, but believing." And Thomas answered and said to Him, "My Lord and my God!"* (John 20:27, 28).

*Let this mind be in you which was also in Christ Jesus, who being in the form of God, did not consider it robbery to be equal with God, but made Himself of no reputation, taking the form of a servant, and coming in the likeness of men* (Philippians 2:5-7).

The reference to "God being manifested in the flesh" obviously refers to Jesus Christ and His incarnation. Further, it refers to His ascension after His resurrection, since it also mentions that He was "received up in glory." Truly, it is a great mystery!

Thomas' confession of Christ's deity mirrors that of his fellow-apostles. They joyfully spread the good news of salvation to the corners of the then-known world, and most gave their lives to proclaim the message.

Hark, the herald angels sing, "Glory to the newborn King!
Peace on earth and mercy mild, God and sinners reconciled."
Joyful all ye nations rise, join the triumph of the skies,
With the angel hosts proclaim,
"Christ is born in Bethlehem!"
Hark, the herald angels sing: "Glory to the newborn King!"

Christ, by highest heaven adored,
Christ, the everlasting Lord.
Late in time behold Him come, offspring of a virgin's womb.
Veiled in flesh the Godhead see, hail the incarnate Deity,
Pleased as man with men to dwell, Jesus, our Emanuel.
Hark, the herald angels sing: "Glory to the newborn King!"

—Charles Wesley

# Be Contented

*Now godliness with contentment is great gain. For we brought nothing into this world, and it is certain that we can carry noting out. And having food and clothing, let us therewith be content. But those who desire to be rich fall into temptation and a snare, and into many foolish and harmful lusts which drown men in destruction and perdition. For the love of money is the root of all kinds of evil, for which some have strayed from the faith in their greediness, and pierced themselves through with many sorrows* (1 Timothy 6:6-10).

Paul had experience with co-workers who got sidetracked by the lure of riches and prestige to be found in other venues. He warned Timothy to stay clear of temptations to enrich himself. He reminded him that he came into the world with nothing and when the time came, he would leave the world again with nothing. He added: "But you, O man of God, flee these things and pursue righteousness, godliness, faith, love, patience, gentleness. Fight the good fight of faith".... (1 Timothy 6:11, 12a). Jesus counseled: "Seek first the kingdom of God and His righteousness, and all these things shall be added to you" (Matthew 6:33).

> Jehovah's perfect law restores the soul again;
> His testimony sure gives wisdom unto men;
> The precepts of the Lord are right,
> And fill the heart with great delight.
>
> The Lord's commands are pure, they light and joy restore;
> Jehovah's fear is clean, enduring evermore;
> His statutes, let the world confess,
> Are wholly truth and righteousness.
>
> They are to be desired above the finest gold,
> Than honey from the comb, more sweetness far they hold.
> With warnings they Thy servant guard,
> In keeping them is great reward.
>
> When Thou dost search my life, may all my thoughts within
> And all the words I speak Thy full approval win....
>
> —Psalter 38, Psalm 19

# God's Endowment

*God has not given us a spirit of fear, but of power and of love and of a sound mind. Therefore do not be ashamed of the testimony of our Lord, nor of me His prisoner, but share with me in the sufferings for the gospel according to the power of God, who has saved us and called us with a holy calling, not according to our works, but according to His own purpose and grace which was given to us before time began* (2 Timothy 1:8, 9).

Since we are about two centuries removed from the writer of this epistle, it is hard to visualize the risks Paul's companions took in order to assist him while he was imprisoned in Rome, awaiting his sentence from Caesar. Although Paul was in chains for the gospel, he affirmed that he "was not ashamed, for I know whom I have believed, and am persuaded that He is able to keep what I have committed to Him until that Day" (2 Timothy 1:12).

Paul grieved that his former friends in Asia had "all turned away from me, among whom are Phygellus and Hermogenes" (verse 15). He gratefully mentioned a visit from Onesiphorus, who "zealously sought me out and found me" (verse 17). He added, "and was not ashamed of my chains."

Jesus called those persecuted for righteousness sake "blessed," for "of such is the kingdom of heaven" (Matthew 5:10).

> In the hour of trial, Jesus, plead for me,
> Lest by base denial, I depart from Thee;
> When Thou seest me waver, with a look recall,
> Not for fear or favor, suffer me to fall.

> With forbidden pleasures would this vain world charm,
> Or its sordid treasures spread to work me harm,
> Bring to my remembrance sad Gethsemane,
> Or with darker semblance, cross-crowned Calvary.

> Should Thy mercy send me, sorrow, toil, or woe,
> Or should pain attend me, on my path below,
> Grant that I may never fail Thy hand to see,
> Grant that I may ever cast my care on Thee.

—James Montgomery

# Qualities of God's Servants

*But avoid foolish and ignorant disputes, knowing that they generate strife. And a servant of the Lord must not quarrel but be gentle to all, able to teach, patient. In humility correcting those who are in opposition, if God perhaps will grant them repentance so that they may know the truth and that they may come to their senses and escape the snare of the devil....* (2 Timothy 2:24-26a).

It is not only pastors who need to be "gentle, able to teach, and patient," but all believers who must interact with argumentative persons. Paul urged Timothy to "correct" the erring person "with humility" in the hope that they may recognize their error.

Remember Jesus' prayer: "I do not pray for these alone, but for all those who will believe on Me through their word; that they may all be one, as You, Father, are in Me, and I in You, that they also may be one in Us, that the world may believe that You sent Me" (John 17:20, 21). The unity of believers makes the gospel message more credible.

Speed Thy servants, Savior, speed them,
Thou art Lord of winds and waves;
They were bound, but Thou hast freed them,
Now they go to free the slaves.
O be with them, 'tis Thine arm alone that saves.

Friends and homes and all forsaking,
Lord, they go at Thy command;
As their stay Thy promise taking,
While they traverse sea and land.
O be with them, lead them safely by the hand.

In the midst of opposition
Let them trust, O Lord in Thee;
When success attains their mission,
Let Thy servants humbler be.
Never leave them, till Thy face in heaven they see.

—Thomas Kelly

# Characteristics of the "Last Days"

*But know this, that in the last days perilous times will come; for men will be lovers of themselves, lovers of money, boasters, proud, blasphemers, disobedient to parents, unthankful, unholy, unloving, unforgiving, slanderers, without self-control, brutal, despisers of good, traitors, headstrong, haughty, lovers of pleasure rather than lovers of God, having a form of godliness but denying its power. And from such people turn away* (2 Timothy 3:1-5)*!*

Paul painted a bleak picture of what unbelievers will be like during the "last days" before Christ returns in triumph. His advice to young Timothy was to avoid them when possible.

Jesus warned his disciples that many deceivers would come and claim to be the Christ, and there will be many false prophets. He added, "Because lawlessness will abound, the love of many will grow cold. But he who endures to the end shall be saved. And this gospel of the kingdom will be preached in all the world, as a witness to all the nations, and then the end will come" (Matthew 24:5, 1-13).

> Make haste, O my God, to deliver, I pray,
> O God, to my rescue make haste;
> Let those who would harm me be filled with dismay,
> And in their own folly disgraced.
>
> Let them be turned back in confusion, O Lord,
> Who in my destruction would joy;
> Let shame and defeat be their only reward
> Who sneers and derision employ.
>
> I cry in deep need and Thy help I implore;
> Make haste to the rescue, I pray;
> My Savior thou art, and my strength evermore,
> No longer Thy coming delay.
>
> May all those who seek Thee and make Thee their choice,
> Great gladness and blessedness see; ...

—Psalter 188, Psalm 70

# Paul Charged Timothy to Be Faithful

*I charge you, therefore,... Preach the word! Be ready in season and out of season. Convince, rebuke, exhort, with all longsuffering and teaching. For the time will come when they will not endure sound doctrine, but according to their own desires, because they have itching ears, they will heap up for themselves teachers, and they will turn away from the truth, and be turned aside to fables* (2 Timothy 4:1a, 2-4).

In the preceding passage Paul showed Timothy how important it was to preach the word, because "all Scripture is given by inspiration of God, and is profitable for doctrine, for reproof, for correction, for instruction in righteousness, that the man of God may be complete, thoroughly equipped for every good work" (2 Timothy 3:16, 17). To protect his flock from rampant error, it was important that Timothy preach the word faithfully and at all times.

Reminding Timothy that his own ministry was nearing its end, Paul was able to testify to his young colleague: "I have fought the good fight, I have finished the race, I have kept the faith" (2 Timothy 4:7).

Will you be able to say the same when the time comes to render an account of your ministry? Remember: "Fight the good fight of faith; lay hold of eternal life" (1 Timothy 6:12).

Thy promised mercies send to me, Thy great salvation, Lord;
So shall I answer those who scoff: my trust is in Thy word.

My hope is in Thy judgment, Lord;
Take not Thy truth from me.
And in Thy law forevermore my daily walk shall be.

And I will walk at liberty, because Thy truth I seek;
Thy truth before the kings of earth with boldness I will speak.

The Lord's commands, which I have loved,
Shall still new joy impart;
With reverence I will hear Thy laws,
And keep them in my heart.

—Psalter 326, Psalm 119

# Paul's Declaration of Faith

*For I am not ashamed of the gospel of Christ, for it is the power of God to salvation for everyone who believes, for the Jew first, and also for the Greek; for in it the righteousness of God is revealed from faith to faith, as it is written, "The just shall live by faith"* (Romans 1:16, 17).

In this first chapter Paul showed that God has sufficiently revealed Himself in nature that no one can plead complete ignorance of Him. It is because men have chosen not to recognize Him that they have developed all types of obscene practices rather than to worship the one true God Who has revealed Himself in nature (Romans 1:18-20). In consequence, they are, Paul wrote "without excuse" (Romans 1:20). God has already pronounced His judgment against those who practice unrighteousness, and are "deserving of death, and who not only do the same, but also approve of those who practice them" (Romans 1:29-32).

In the second chapter, Paul turned to the people who know the law and condemn these obscene practices in others, but committed many themselves. He affirmed that they will not escape God's wrath on the day of judgment. Just knowing the law will not excuse those who do evil (Romans 2:5, 6, 9).

Lord, I believe; Thy power I own, Thy word I would obey;
I wander comfortless and lone when from Thy truth I stray.

Lord, I believe, but gloomy fears
Sometimes bedim my sight;
I look to Thee with prayers and tears,
And cry for strength and light.

Lord, I believe, but Thou dost know
My faith is cold and weak.
Pity my frailty and bestow the confidence I seek.

Lord, I believe, and only Thou
Canst give my soul relief;
Lord, to Thy truth my spirit bow;
Help Thou mine unbelief.

—J. R. Wreford

# All Are Equally Guilty

*There is no partiality with God. For as many as have sinned without law will also perish without law, and as many as have sinned in the law will be judged by the law* (Romans 2:11, 12).... *Therefore by the deeds of the law no flesh will be justified in His sight, for by the law is the knowledge of sin. But now the righteousness of God apart from the law is revealed, being witnessed by the Law and the Prophets, even the righteousness of God through faith in Jesus Christ, to all and on all who believe. For there is no difference: for all have sinned and fall short of the glory of God* (Romans 3:20-23).

The Jews believed that their expertise in God's law made them acceptable to God, but Paul, who was himself a Jew, reminded them that knowing the law was insufficient; they needed to obey all the laws perfectly, and this no human being was able to do.

Those who believe on Jesus Christ and His finished work of redemption on the cross on their behalf are justified by faith. He demonstrated this from the Old Testament patriarch Abraham, who believed God, and it was accounted to him for righteousness (Genesis 15:6).

Rock of Ages, cleft for me, let me hide myself in Thee;
Let the water and the blood
From Thy wounded side which flowed,
Be of sin the double cure,
Cleanse me from its guilt and power.

Not the labor of my hands can fulfill Thy laws demands;
Could my zeal no respite know,
Could my tears forever flow,
All for sin could not atone; Thou must save, and Thou alone.

Nothing in my hand I bring, simply to Thy cross I cling;
Naked, come to Thee for dress,
Helpless, look to Thee for grace;
Foul, I to the fountain fly; wash me, Savior, or I die.

—Augustus M. Toplady

# More on Justification by Faith

*Therefore we conclude that a man is justified by faith apart from the deeds of the law. Or is He the God of the Jews only? Is He not also the God of the Gentiles? Yes, of the Gentiles also, since there is one God who will justify the circumcised by faith and the uncircumcised through faith. Do we then make void the law through faith? Certainly not! On the contrary, we establish the law* (Romans 3:28-31).

In the chapter that follows these verses, Paul proves his point that justification is by faith, not by works, by quoting the passages in the Old Testament that affirm that the patriarch Abraham was justified by faith, and not by keeping the law, which was not given to Israel until several centuries later. Abraham himself was not even circumcised until later. Therefore, he was justified by believing God, not by being circumcised.

Paul summarized his explanation by affirming: "Therefore, being justified by faith, we have peace with God through our Lord Jesus Christ, through whom we have access by faith into this grace in which we stand, and rejoice in the hope of the glory of God" (Romans 5:1, 2).

Truly, God's grace is amazing! By faith we may have access to the very throne-room of God, through our Lord Jesus Christ, who died on the cross in our stead.

> I am trusting Thee, Lord Jesus, trusting only Thee;
> Trusting Thee for full salvation, great and free.
>
> I am trusting Thee for pardon, at Thy feet I bow;
> For Thy grace and tender mercy, trusting now.
>
> I am trusting Thee for cleansing
> In the crimson flood;
> Trusting Thee to make me holy by Thy blood.
>
> I am trusting Thee to guide me;
> Thou alone shalt lead;
> Every day and hour supplying all my need.

—Frances R. Havergal

# God's Faithful Love

*O wretched man that I am! Who will deliver me from this body of death? I thank God—through Jesus Christ our Lord! So then, with the mind I serve the law of God, but with the flesh the law of sin.*

*There is therefore now no condemnation to those who are in Christ Jesus, who do not walk according to the flesh, but according to the Spirit. For the law of the Spirit of life in Christ Jesus has made me free from the law of sin and death* (Romans 7:24, 25; 8:1).

In the preceding verses of chapter 7, Paul decried his tendencies to sin in spite of his longing to serve God with all his heart. He wrote: "For what I am doing, I do not understand. For what I will to do, that I do not practice, but what I hate, that I do. If, then, I do what I will not to do, I agree with the law that it is good…. For I know that in me (that is, in my flesh) nothing good dwells, for to will is present with me, but how to perform what is good I do not find" (Romans 7:15, 16, 18).

Free from the law, O happy condition,
Jesus hath bled, and there is remission;
Cursed by the law and bruised by the fall,
Grace hath redeemed us once for all.

Now we are free—there's no condemnation,
Jesus provides a perfect salvation;
"Come unto Me," O hear His sweet call,
Come, and He saves us once for all.

"Children of God," O glorious calling,
Surely His grace will keep us from falling;
Passing from death to life at His call,
Blessed salvation, once for all.

Once for all, O sinner, receive it,
Once for all, O brother, believe it;
Cling to the cross, the burden will fall;
Christ has redeemed us, once for all!

—Philip P. Bliss

# We Are United with Christ

*Therefore we were buried with Him through baptism into death, that just as Christ was raised from the dead by the glory of the Father, even so we also should walk in newness of life. For if we have been united together in the likeness of His death, certainly we also shall be in the likeness of His resurrection* (Romans 6:4, 5).

As Paul explained the certainty of our physical resurrection, he showed that it is guaranteed along with Jesus' physical death on the cross and His resurrection.

In the fifteenth chapter of First Corinthians he goes into this guarantee in great detail. He wrote: "For I delivered to you first of all that which I also received; that Christ died for our sins according to the Scriptures, and that He was buried and that He rose again the third day according to the Scriptures, ... Now if Christ is preached as being raised from the dead, how do some among you say that there is no resurrection of the dead? But if there is no resurrection of the dead, then Christ is not risen. And if Christ is not risen, your faith is futile, you are still in your sins" (1 Corinthians 15:3, 4, 12-14).

Jesus lives, and so shall I; death, thy sting is gone forever!
He for me has deigned to die,
Lives the bands of death to sever.
He shall raise me from the dust; Jesus is my hope and trust.

And His Kingdom still remaining,
I shall also be with Him, ever living, ever reigning.
Jesus lives and reigns supreme;
God has promised—be it must; Jesus is my hope and trust.

Jesus lives and death is now but my entrance into glory;
Courage, then, my soul, for thou
Hast a crown of life before thee.
Thou shalt find thy hopes were just:
Jesus is thy hope and trust.

—Christian F. Gellert, trans. Philip Schaff

# Wages vs. Gift

*What fruit did you have then in the things of which you are now ashamed? For the end of these things is death. But now having been set free from sin, and having become slaves of God, you have your fruit to holiness, and the end, everlasting life. For the wages of sin is death, but the gift of God is eternal life in Jesus Christ our Lord* (Romans 6: 21-25).

Paul sums up his exposition of God's gift of grace with a powerful statement: "The wages of sin is death, but the gift of God is eternal life in Jesus Christ our Lord."

My sister-in-law—a minister's wife—on her death bed, simply pleaded: "My Jesus, I love thee, I know Thou art mine."

Dear friend, the author of the poem below stated very simply her own faith based on John 6:37, 39: "All that the Father gives Me will come to Me, and the one who comes to Me I will by no means cast out.... And this is the will of Him who sent Me, that everyone who sees the Son and believes in Him may have everlasting life; and I will raise him up at the last day."

On this promise from one who cannot fail and cannot lie, I rest my faith for eternity. Paul wrote: "What then shall we say to these things? If God be for us, who can be against us" (Romans 8:31, 32)?

My faith has found a resting place, not in device or creed;
I trust the ever living One, His wounds for me shall plead.

Enough for me that Jesus saves, this ends my fears and doubt;
A sinful soul, I came to Him, He'll never cast me out.

My heart is leaning on the Word, the written Word of God;
Salvation by my Savior's name, salvation through His blood.

I need no other argument, I need no other plea;
It is enough that Jesus died, and that He died for me.

—Lidie H. Edmunds

# Faith in a Master Who Was Asleep

*Now when He got into a boat His disciples followed Him. And suddenly a great tempest arose on the sea, so that the boat was covered with waves. But He was asleep.*

*Then His disciples came to Him and awoke Him, saying, "Lord, save us! We are perishing!" But He said to them, "Why are your fearful, O you of little faith?" Then He arose and rebuked the winds and sea, and there was a great calm* (Matthew 8:23-26).

Jesus' disciples were terrorized by a storm that arose suddenly and threatened to swamp the boat. The fact that they woke Jesus from His sleep shows that they expected Him to save them from the elements, but they apparently thought that He would not be able to do so if He were asleep.

The fact that they called on Him to save them proved that they believed in Him, but not enough to be at peace in a storm, with the Master asleep.

Friend, do you trust the Lord in the storms of your life? Do you trust Him even if He seems asleep?

Simply trusting every day, trusting through a stormy way,
Even when my faith is small; trusting Jesus, that is all.

Brightly does His Spirit shine into this poor heart of mine;
While He leads, I cannot fall; trusting Jesus, that is all.

Singing if my way is clear, praying, if the path is drear;
If in danger, for Him call; trusting Jesus, that is all.

Trusting Him while life shall last,
Trusting Him till earth be past,
Till within the jasper wall, trusting Jesus, that is all,

Trusting as the moments fly,
Trusting as the days go by;
Trusting Him whate'er befall,
Trusting Jesus, that is all.

—Edgar P. Sites

# The Preciousness of the Cross

*But God forbid that I should boast except in the cross of our Lord Jesus Christ, by whom the world has been crucified to me, and I to the world* (Galatians 6:14).

*For He Himself* [Christ] *is our peace, who has made both one, and has broken down the middle wall of separation... For through Him we both have access by one Spirit to the Father* (Ephesians 2:14, 18).

Paul points out that the cross both divides and unites. It divides believers from unbelievers, and it unites all believers—whatever their ethnic or racial background—into a single body: the universal Church, the body of Christ.

Jesus prayed: "That they all may be one, as You, Father, are in Me, and I in You; that they may be one in Us, that the world may believe that You sent Me" (John 17:21). The unity of those professing the Name of Christ is a powerful message to the world. In spite of the many "labels" that divide us, let us demonstrate the reconciliation of the cross to our world.

Jesus, keep me near the cross, there a precious fountain,
Free to all, a healing stream
Flows from Calvary's mountain.

In the cross, a trembling soul, love and mercy found me,
There the bright and morning Star
Shed its beams around me.

Near the cross, O Lamb of God, bring its scenes before me,
Help me walk from day to day
With its shadows o'er me.

Near the cross I'll watch and wait, hoping, trusting ever,
Till I reach the golden strand
Just beyond the river.

In the cross, in the cross, be my glory ever,
Till my ransomed soul shall find rest beyond the river.

—Fanny J. Crosby

# Righteousness by Faith

*But now the righteousness of God apart from the law is revealed, being witnessed by the Law and the Prophets, even the righteousness of God, through faith in Jesus Christ, to all and on all who believe. For there is no difference, for all have sinned and fall short of the glory of God, being justified freely by His grace through the redemption that is in Christ Jesus...*(Romans 3:21-24)

The apostle Paul is emphatic in his reassurance that salvation is entirely by grace and not by any works or effort of ours. When we realize that we are far from attaining God's standard of righteousness, it is a great comfort to remember that He has "justified us freely by His grace through the redemption that is in Christ Jesus."

Paul went on to assure the Roman believers: "Therefore we were buried with Him through baptism into death, that just as Christ was raised from the dead by the glory of the Father, even so we also should walk in the newness of life. For if we have been united together in the likeness of His death, certainly we also shall be in the likeness of His resurrection" (Romans 6:4, 5).

> Tell me the old, old story of unseen things above,
> Of Jesus and His glory, of Jesus and His love;
> Tell me the story simply as to a little child,
> For I am weak and weary,
> And helpless and defiled.
>
> Tell me the story slowly that I may take it in,
> That wonderful redemption, God's remedy for sin.
> Tell me the story often, for I forget so soon;
> The early dew of morning
> Has passed away at noon.
>
> Tell me the same old story when you have cause to fear
> That this world's empty glory is costing me too dear;
> Tell the story always, if you would really be
> In any time of trouble
> A comforter to me.

—A. Catherine Hankey

# Living by Faith

*For the law of the Spirit of life in Christ Jesus has made me free from the law of sin and death. For what the law could not do in that it was weak through the flesh, God did by sending His own Son in the likeness of sinful flesh on account of sin: He condemned sin in the flesh...He* [God] *who did not spare His own Son, but delivered Him up for us all, how shall He not with Him also freely give us all things* (Romans 8:2-3, 32)?

Paul reminded us that when God gave His own beloved Son for our salvation, He gave us His all, and will not withhold any blessings from us.

Dear friend, James wrote: "Every good gift, and every perfect gift is from above, and comes down from the Father of lights, with whom there is no variation or shadow of turning" (James 1:17). Since God does not change, His promises are always valid and trustworthy.

"Thanks be to God for His indescribable gift" (2 Corinthians 9:15)!

> O Jesus, I have promised to serve Thee to the end;
> Be Thou forever near me, my Master and my Friend;
> I shall not fear the battle if Thou are by my side,
>    Nor wander from the pathway,
>    If Thou wilt be my guide.
>
> O let me feel Thee near me; the world is ever near,
> I see the lights that dazzle, the tempting sounds I hear—
> My foes are ever near me, around me and within;
>    But Jesus, draw Thou nearer,
>    And shield my soul from sin.
>
> O Jesus, Thou hast promised to all who follow Thee,
> That where Thou art in glory, there shall Thy servant be;
> And Jesus, I have promised to serve Thee to the end;
>    O give me grace to follow
>    My Master and my Friend.

—John E. Bode

# The Message of Faith

*If you confess with your mouth the Lord Jesus and believe in your heart that God has raised Him from the dead, you will be saved. For with the heart one believes unto righteousness, and with the mouth confession is made unto salvation. For the Scripture says, "Whoever believes on Him will not be put to shame"* (Romans 10:9-11).

Paul supported his thesis on salvation by faith, by quoting from the Old Testament prophet Isaiah 28:16: "Behold, I lay in Zion a stone for a foundation, a tried stone, a precious cornerstone, a sure foundation. Whoever believes will not act hastily."

When Peter and John defended their healing of the lame man in the temple, Peter cited the same verse: "Let it be known to you all, and by all the people of Israel, that by the name of Jesus Christ of Nazareth, whom you crucified, whom God raised from the dead, by Him this man stands here before you whole. This is the stone which was rejected by you builders, which has become the chief cornerstone. Nor is there salvation in any other, for there is no other name under heaven given among men by which we must be saved" (Acts 4:10-12).

> My only hope must be in Jesus,
> Who made atonement for my sin;
> There is no other one can help me,
> Alone in Christ I must begin.
>
> My only hope must be in Jesus,
> For cleansing by His precious blood;
> My faith must build upon His promise—
> Whose truth all trial has withstood.
>
> There is no other Savior given,
> No other hope beyond the grave,
> No other name in earth or heaven
> My guilty, dying soul, could save.
>
> —Ina Duley Ogdon

# Salvation Is on an Equal Basis

*And it shall come to pass that whoever calls on the name of the LORD shall be saved. For in Mount Zion and in Jerusalem there shall be deliverance, as the LORD has said, among the remnant whom the LORD calls* (Joel 2:32).

*For there is no distinction between Jew and Greek, for the same Lord over all is rich to all who call upon Him. For whoever calls on the name of the Lord shall be saved* (Romans 10:12, 13).

The apostle Paul cites the prophesy of Joel, to prove that salvation is by faith for all who call upon the Lord, independent of whether they are Jews or Gentiles.

In the psalm below we are urged to spread this wonderful and universal gospel throughout the world that has not yet heard this glorious message. God is no respecter of persons nor does He value one ethic group over another.

As Jesus explained to the Pharisee Nicodemus, "God so loved the world, that He gave His only begotten Son, that whoever believes in Him should not perish, but have everlasting life. For God did not send His Son into the world to condemn the world, but that the world through Him might be saved" (John 3:16, 17).

Sing to the Lord, sing His praise, all ye peoples,
New be your song as new honors ye pay;
Sing of His majesty, bless Him forever,
Show His salvation from day to day.

Tell of His wondrous works, tell of His glory,
Till through the nations His Name is revered;
Praise and exalt Him, for He is almighty;
God over all let the Lord be feared.

Make all the nations know God reigns forever,
Earth is established as He did decree;
Righteous and just is the King of the nations,
Judging the people with equity.

—Psalter 259, Psalm 76

# Faith Through Hearing God's Word

*So then faith comes by hearing, and hearing by the word of God.... But Isaiah is very bold and says, "I was found by those who did not seek Me; I was made manifest to those who did not ask for Me"* (Romans 10:17, 20, quoting Isaiah: *I was sought by those who did not ask for Me; I was found by those who did not seek Me. I said "Here I am, here I am," to a nation that was not called by My name* (Isaiah 65:1).

Paul explained that the gospel invitation to the Gentile world was already proclaimed by the Old Testament prophets. We know that the salvation of the Gentiles was not a divine afterthought, because God already made this clear when He called Abraham from Ur of the Chaldeans: "In you all the families of the earth will be blessed" (Genesis 12:3b).

In the last book of the Bible, in the final chapter, Jesus repeats his invitation to anyone who "thirsts": "Let him who thirsts come. Whoever desires, let him take the water of life freely" (Revelation 22:17).

> The cross upon which Jesus died
> Is a shelter in which we can hide;
> And His grace is so free; it's sufficient for me,
> And deep is its fountain, as wide as the sea.
>
> Though millions have found Him a friend,
> And turned from the sins they have sinned;
> The Savior still waits to open the gate,
> And welcome the sinner, before it's too late.
>
> The hand of my Savior is strong,
> And the love of my Savior is long:
> Through sunshine or rain, through loss or through gain,
> The blood flows from Calvary to cleanse every stain.
>
> Though millions have come, there's still room for one;
> Yes, there's room at the cross for you.

—Ira F. Stanphill

# God's Wisdom Is Unsearchable

*For God has committed them all to disobedience, that He might have mercy on all. Oh, the depth of the riches both of the wisdom and knowledge of God! How unsearchable are His judgments and His ways past finding out! For who has known the mind of the LORD? Or who has become His counselor* (Romans 11:32-34)?

Paul paused in his exposition of God's amazing grace to a world of lost sinners, whether Jew or Gentile, to utter this eulogy of praise. God's grace is beyond our understanding. His love is eternal, and His mercy extends to all human societies.

An unknown psalmist invited the Gentiles to join in praising the Lord: "Praise the LORD, all you Gentiles! Laud Him, all you peoples! For His merciful kindness is great toward us, and the truth of the LORD endures forever" (Psalm 117).

Dear friend, eternity will not be too long to praise our great Redeemer for the grace and love He has extended to us. Nothing and no one "can separate us from the love of God which is in Christ Jesus our Lord" (Romans 8:38, 39).

> My God, how wonderful Thou art!
> Thy majesty, how bright!
> How beautiful Thy mercy-seat,
> In depths of burning light!
>
> O how I fear Thee, living God,
> With deepest, tenderest fears!
> And worship Thee with trembling hope,
> And penitential tears.
>
> Yet I may love Thee, too, O Lord,
> Almighty as Thou art,
> For Thou hast stooped to ask of me
> The love of my poor heart.
>
> Father of Jesus, love's reward,
> What rapture will it be
> Prostrate before Thy throne to lie,
> And gaze and gaze on Thee!
>
> —Frederick W. Faber

# We Are to Be "Living Sacrifices"

[Paul wrote:] *I beseech you, therefore, brethren, by the mercies of God, that you present your bodies a living sacrifice, holy, acceptable to God, which is your reasonable service. And do not be conformed to the world, but be transformed by the renewing of your mind, that you may prove what is that good and perfect will of God* (Romans 12:1, 2).

God has given us His best—His own beloved Son—then it is "reasonable" to give ourselves wholeheartedly to Him, although we are scarred by sin and prone to wander. When we do this, we open ourselves to His renewal of our minds, and the process of becoming more like our Savior.

Paul went on to explain what this "renewal" would be like: "Let love be without hypocrisy. Abhor what is evil, cling to what is good. Be kindly affectionate to one another with brotherly love, in honor giving preference to one another, not lagging in diligence, fervent in sprit, serving the Lord, rejoicing in hope, patient in tribulation, continuing steadfastly in prayer.... If it is possible, as much as depends on you, live peaceably with all men," and "do not avenge yourselves" (Romans 12:9-12, 18).

I am Thine, O Lord, I have heard Thy voice,
And it told Thy love to me;
But I long to rise in the arms of love
And be closer drawn to Thee.

Consecrate me now, to Thy service, Lord,
By the power of grace divine;
Let my soul look up with a steadfast hope,
And my will be lost in Thine.

There are depths of love that I cannot know
Till I cross the narrow sea;
There are heights of joy that I cannot reach,
Till I rest in peace with Thee.

—Fanny J. Crosby

149

# God Will Avenge our Wrongs

[Paul wrote:] *Beloved, do not avenge yourselves, but rather give place to wrath, for it is written, "Vengeance is Mine; I will repay," says the Lord. Therefore, "If your enemy is hungry, feed him; if he is thirsty, give him a drink; for in so doing you will heap coals of fire on his head"* (Romans 12:19-20).

Paul quotes Solomon and Jesus Himself as he urges us to do good to those who persecute us.

Not only will our kindness to them put them to shame, but it may cause them to change their minds about Christians. And above all, it may make our enemy receptive to the gospel. It is hard to hate someone who shows you a kindness.

Notice that God retains the right to wreak judgment on the wicked. He has never granted us this right. Jesus was silent when He was mocked and beaten, and He calls us to walk in His footsteps (1 Peter 3:21).

Sweetly, Lord, have we heard Thee calling,
Come, follow Me!"
And we see where Thy footprints falling
Lead us to Thee.

Though they lead o'er the cold, dark mountains,
Seeking His sheep,
Or along by Siloam's fountains,
Helping the weak.

If they lead through the temple holy,
Preaching the Word,
Or in homes of the poor and lowly,
Serving the Lord.

Footprints of Jesus that make the pathway glow!
We will follow the steps of Jesus
Where'er they go.

—Mary B. C. Slade

# Fulfilling Six Commandments

*Owe no one anything, except to love one another, for he who loves another has fulfilled the law. For the commandments, "You shall not commit adultery,' "You shall not murder," "You shall not steal," "You shall not bear false witness," "You shall not covet," and if there is any other commandment, are all summed up in this saying, namely, "You shall love your neighbor as yourself."*

*Love does no harm to a neighbor, therefore love is the fulfillment of the law* (Romans 13:8-10).

Paul summarized the six commandments that deal with our behavior to others, and concluded that they epitomized love to others by seeking the best for them. In this he joined Jesus, who expounded the need to love our enemies: "But I say to you who hear, love your enemies, do good to those who hate you, bless those who curse you and pray for those who spitefully use you" because our heavenly Father showers his blessings on the wicked as well as the just (Luke 6:27-36). He illustrated this message in the well-known parable of the Good Samaritan, Luke 10:24-31.

I found that while we have some hymns that promote love to other Christians (see below), we seem to have very few broad enough to include just anyone who is in need, as Jesus defined the term "neighbor." He asked the lawyer, "So which of these three do you think was neighbor go him who fell among the thieves?" And the lawyer answered, "He who showed mercy on him" Jesus replied, "Go and do likewise" (Luke 10:36, 37).

> In Christ there is no East or West,
> In Him, no South or North;
> But one great fellowship of love
> Throughout the whole wide earth.
>
> Join hands, then, brothers of the faith,
> Whate'er your race may be;
> Who serves my Father as a son
> Is surely kin to me.
>
> —John Oxenham

# Respect Your Brother's Conscience

*Let us not judge one another anymore, but rather resolve this, not to put a stumbling block, or a cause to fall in our brother's way.... Do not destroy the work of God for the sake of food. All things indeed are pure, but it is evil for the man who eats with offense... for whatever is not from faith is sin* (Romans 14:13, 20, 23).

Although Paul uses the example of taboo foods in this chapter, it could refer to any debatable practice. The main point of this chapter is that we must be careful to consider a brother's qualms in such cases. We must restrain ourselves from doing anything that our brother considers wrong, because if he should be encouraged to follow our example although he considers it wrong, it would make him feel guilty.

Paul insisted that, as the stronger brother, we must defer to our brother's qualms in matters of debatable issues. Instead of trying to convince him to share our view of the practice, we should respect his, and restrain ourselves out of love for our brother. (Romans 15:1).

O Master, let me walk with Thee
In lowly paths of service free,
Tell me Thy secret—help me bear
The strain of toil, the fret of care.

Help me the slow of heart to move
By some clear winning word of love,
Teach me the wayward feet to stay
And guide them in the homeward way.

Teach me Thy patience! Still with Thee
In closer, dearer company;
In work that keeps faith sweet and strong,
In trust that triumphs over wrong....

In peace that only Thou canst give,
With Thee, O Master, let me live.

—Washington Gladden

# Be Like-Minded Towards Each Other

*For whatever things were written before were written for our learning, that we through the patience and comfort of the Scripture might have hope.*

*Now may the God of patience and comfort grant you to be like-minded toward one another, according to Christ Jesus* (Romans 15:4, 5).

After quoting many Old Testament sources in the previous chapters, Paul reminded the Romans that these scriptures were written for their benefit, as well as for those who lived in Old Testament era.

With this in mind, Paul urged the Roman Christians to strive to agree among themselves, so that they might demonstrate the love of Christ to the unbelieving world. Jesus had prayed: "I do not pray for these alone, but also for those who will believe in Me through their word, that they all may be one as You, Father, are in Me, and I in You; that they also may be one in Us, that the world may believe that You sent Me" (John 17:20, 21).

O Word of God Incarnate, O Wisdom from on high,
O Truth unchanged, unchanging, O Light of our dark sky;
We praise Thee for the radiance that from the hallowed page,
A lantern for our footsteps, shines on from age to age.

The Church from her dear Master received the gift divine,
And still that light she lifteth o'er all the earth to shine.
It is the golden casket where gems of truth are stored,
It is the heaven drawn picture of Christ, the living Word....

It is the chart and compass that o'er life's surging sea,
Mid mists and rocks and quicksands,
Still guides O Christ to Thee.

O make Thy Church, dear Savior, a lamp of purest gold;
To bear before the nations Thy true light as of old.
O teach Thy wandering pilgrims by this their path to trace,
Till clouds and darkness ended, they see Thee face to face.

—William W. How

# Accept Other Races

*Therefore receive one another, just as Christ also received us, to the glory of God.... And that the Gentiles might glorify God for His mercy, as it is written; "For this reason I will confess to you among the Gentiles and sing to Your name* (Romans 15:7, 9).

Paul quoted Psalm 18:49 as he encouraged the Gentile converts in Rome: "Therefore I will give thanks to You, O LORD, among the Gentiles, and sing praises to Your name."

Paul, the apostle among the Gentiles, knew well the Old Testament prophesies that related to the evangelism of the non-Jewish populations of the known world, and rejoiced with them in the open doors to the Gentiles. Today we are accustomed to thinking of Gentile believers as genuine Christians. Now we need to adjust ourselves to recall that God has not permanently rejected the descendants of Abraham, Isaac, and Jacob. The day coming—it may be dawning now—when there will be a massive turning to the true Messiah on the part of the Jewish people (Romans 11:25-27). Let us join in praising God for His mercy and faithfulness.

Meanwhile, let us welcome believers from all races and traditions to the family of God.

All nations, clap your hands,
Let shouts of triumph ring,
For mighty over all the lands,
The Lord Most High is King.

O sing in joyful strains,
And make His glory known,
God over all the nations reigns,
And holy is His throne.

Our fathers' God to own
The kings of earth draw nigh,
For none can save but God alone,
His is the Lord Most High.

—Psalter 130, Psalm 47

154

# Avoid Trouble-Makers

*Now I urge you, brethren, note those who cause divisions and offenses, contrary to the doctrine which you learned, and avoid them. For those who are such do not serve our Lord Jesus Christ, but their own belly, and by smooth words and flattering speech deceive the hearts of the simple. For your obedience has become known to all. Therefore I am glad on your behalf, but I want you to be wise in what is good, and simple concerning evil* (Romans 16:17-19).

Paul's concern for the Roman Church was that the people would accept all professing believers at face value, including those who were sowing discord in the fellowship. New believers easily become the targets for nominal Christians who try to cause problems in the Church, merely to raise their own esteem.

Paul concluded his epistle with this warning after transmitting greetings from his colleagues.

An unknown psalmist composed the following psalm, teaching us how to avoid this ego trap: by focusing on God's law. Skirt the debatable issues, and concentrate on what God has revealed to be His will for us.

> Blest is he who loves God's precepts,
> Who from sin restrains his feet,
> He who will not stand with sinners,
> He who shuns the scorners' seat.
>
> Blest is he who makes the statutes
> Of the Lord his chief delight;
> In God's law, divinely perfect
> Meditating day and night.
>
> Well the Lord will guard the righteous,
> For their way to Him is known;
> But the way of evil-doers
> Shall by Him be overthrown.

—Psalter 2, Psalm 1

# Justified by Faith Alone

[Paul wrote:] *We who are Jews by nature, and not sinners of the Gentiles, knowing that a man is not justified by the works of the law but by faith in Jesus Christ, even we have believed in Christ Jesus, that we might be justified by faith in Christ and not by the works of the law, for by the works of the law no flesh shall be justified* (Galatians 2:15, 16).

Paul affirmed what was to become one of the banners of the Reformation: "Only through Christ's atonement, only by faith in Him, only through grace, only scripture is our guide, only to God be the glory." Salvation is not attained by human efforts, but it is a "gift of God; not of works, lest anyone should boast" (Ephesians 2:8).

Because salvation is only through Christ's mediatorial atonement, Paul could say: "I have been crucified with Christ; it is no longer I who live, but Christ lives in me, and the life which I now live in the flesh, I live by faith in the Son of God, who loved me and gave Himself for me" (Galatians 2:20).

> My hope is built on nothing less
> Than Jesus' blood and righteousness;
> I dare not trust the sweetest frame,
> But wholly lean on Jesus' name.
>
> His oath, His covenant, His blood
> Support me in the whelming flood;
> When all around my soul gives way,
> He then is all my hope and stay.
>
> When He shall come with trumpet sound,
> O may I then in Him be found;
> Dressed in His righteousness alone,
> Faultless to stand before the throne.
>
> On Christ the solid rock I stand—
> All other ground is sinking sand.
>
> —Edward Mote

# All Scripture Promotes Faith

*And the Scripture, foreseeing that God would justify the Gentiles by faith, preached the gospel to Abraham beforehand, saying "In you all the nations shall be blessed." So then those who are of faith are blessed with believing Abraham. But that no one is justified by the law in the sight of God is evident, for "the just shall live by faith"* (Galatians 3:8, 9, 11).

The sons of Korah sang: "I will make mention of Rahab and Babylon to those who know Me. Behold, O Philistia and Tyre, with Ethiopia: 'This one was born there.' And of Zion it will be said, 'This one and that one were born in her; and the Most High Himself shall establish her.' The LORD will record, when He registers the peoples: 'This one was born there.'" (Psalm 87:4-6).

An unknown psalmist sang: "God be merciful to us and bless us, and cause His face to shine upon us that Your way may be known on earth, Your salvation among all nations,... and all the ends of the earth shall fear Him" (Psalm 87:1, 2 ,7).

> Zion, founded on the mountains,
> God, thy Maker, loves thee well;
> He has chosen thee, most precious,
> He delights in thee to dwell;
> God's own city, who can all thy glories tell?
>
> Heathen lands and hostile people
> Soon shall come the Lord to know;
> Nations born again in Zion
> Shall the Lord's salvation show,
> God Almighty shall on Zion strength bestow.
>
> When the Lord shall count the nations,
> Sons and daughters He shall see,
> Born to endless life in Zion,
> And their joyful song shall be,
> "Blessed Zion, all our fountains are in thee."

—Psalter 238, Psalm 87

# In the Fullness of Time....

*When the fullness of time had come, God sent forth His Son, born of a woman, born under the law, to redeem those who were under the law, that we might receive the adoption as sons. And because you are sons, God has sent forth the Spirit of His Son into your hearts crying out, "Abba, Father!" Therefore you are no longer a slave but a son, and if a son, then an heir of God through Christ* (Galatians 4:4-7).

Paul explained the magnitude of God's gifts to mortal sinners. Not only did He restore us to Adam and Eve's status of righteousness, but He determined to adopt these redeemed sinners as His children. He loved us so much that He raised us above the status that our first parents had enjoyed in Eden.

The apostle John wrote: ...as many as received Him, to them He gave the right to become children of God, to those who believe on His name;..." (John 1:11-13).

Paul summarized: "For we through the Spirit eagerly wait for the hope of righteousness by faith. For in Christ Jesus neither circumcision nor uncircumcision avails anything, but faith working through love" (Galatians 5:5, 6).

My Father is rich in houses and lands,
He holdeth the wealth of the world in His hands!
Of rubies and diamonds, of silver and gold,
His coffers are full—He has riches untold.

My Father's own Son, the Savior of men,
Once wandered o'er earth as the poorest of them;
But now He is reigning forever on high,
And will give me a home in heaven by and by.

I once was an outcast stranger on earth,
A sinner by choice and an alien by birth,
But I've been adopted, my name's written down—
An heir to a mansion, a robe, and a crown.

—Harriet E. Buell

# Love Fulfills the Law

*For you, brethren have been called to liberty, only do not use liberty as an opportunity for the flesh, but through love serve one another. For all the law is fulfilled in one word, even in this: "You shall love your neighbor as yourself." But if you bite and devour one another, beware lest you be consumed by one another! I say then, walk in the Spirit, and you shall not fulfill the lust of the flesh* (Galatians 5:13-16).

It appears that the Galatian Christians were indulging in some unspiritual backbiting, which alarmed the apostle Paul. He warned them that such behavior was destructive and urged them to "walk in the Spirit" to avoid such clashes.

In stating that "love is the fulfillment of the law" (Romans 13:10), Paul reminds us of Christ's words (Matthew 5:44). The apostle John urged, "He who loves his brother abides in the light, and there is no cause of stumbling in him. But a man who hates his brother is in darkness and walks in darkness and does not know where he is going, because darkness has blinded his eyes" (1 John 2:10, 11).

Peter called attention to Christ's example: "Who, when He was reviled, did not revile in return; when He suffered, He did not threaten, but committed Himself to Him who judges righteously" (1 Peter 2:23).

> To Thee I lift my soul, in Thee my trust repose;
> My God, O put me not to shame
> Before triumphant foes.
>
> None shall be put to shame that humbly wait for Thee,
> But those that willfully transgress,
> On them the shame shall be.
>
> Show me Thy paths, O Lord; teach me Thy perfect way.
> O guide me in Thy truth divine,
> And lead me day by day.
>
> —Psalter 62, Psalm 25

# Restore Your Fallen Brother

*Brethren, if a man is overtaken in any trespass, you who are spiritual restore such a one in a spirit of gentleness, considering yourself lest you also be tempted.*

*Bear one another's burdens, and so fulfill the law of Christ... Let him who is taught the word share in all good things with him who teaches* (Galatians 6:1, 2, 6).

The apostle Paul ends his epistle with counsel for the young Gentile congregation to enable them to live a Christlike life in the community and in the social context where God has placed them.

First, he warned the leaders to be careful to be gentle with an erring brother. He reminded them that they are also vulnerable to temptation, so treat an erring brother gently, as they would themselves like to be treated. Then he reminded the believers to "bear one another's burdens," because this is a Christlike act of love. He further urged the neophytes to share what they had with their mentors.

Paul closed with his acknowledgment that he owed everything to the cross of our Lord Jesus Christ, "by whom the world has been crucified to me, and I to the world" (Galatians 6:14).

The poet prayed for God's wisdom in communicating with her world:

> Father, I know that all my life is portioned out for me;
> The changes that are sure to come I do not fear to see;
> I ask Thee for a present mind intent on pleasing Thee.

I ask Thee for a thoughtful love, through constant watching wise,
To meet the glad with joyful smiles, to wipe the weeping eyes;
A heart at leisure from itself to soothe and sympathize.

I ask Thee for the daily strength to none that ask denied,
A mind to blend with outward life, while keeping near Thy side,
Content to fill a little space, if Thou be glorified.

—Anna L. Waring

# Don't Kid Yourself

*Do not be deceived, God is not mocked; for whatever a man sows, that he will also reap. For he who sows to his flesh will of the flesh reap corruption, but he who sows to the Spirit will of the Spirit reap everlasting life. And let us not grow weary while doing good, for in due season we shall reap if we do not lose heart. Therefore, as we have opportunity, let us do good to all, especially to those who are of the household of faith* (Galatians 6:7-10).

Finally, Paul warned the Galatian believers that although God's discipline may be delayed, they must not assume that God is indifferent to their errors. God is just, and He will judge their sin appropriately in His time. If we sow weeds we must not expect to reap grain. We will surely reap the type of weeds we have sown.

It is easy to become discouraged when we see no expected results from our good deeds. Some results will only appear in eternity, although others may become apparent in our lifetimes. Let us not lose heart. We do not strive for gratitude on the part of our beneficiaries, but we labor for our Master's "well done!"

> Sowing in the morning, sowing deeds of kindness,
> Sowing in the noontime and the dewy eve;
> Waiting for the harvest, and the time of reaping,
> We shall come rejoicing, bringing in the sheaves.
>
> Sowing in the sunshine, sowing in the shadows,
> Fearing neither clouds nor winter's chilling breeze;
> By and by the harvest, and the time of reaping,
> We shall come rejoicing, bringing in the sheaves.
>
> Going forth with weeping, sowing for the Master,
> Though the loss sustained our spirit often grieves;
> When our weeping's over, He will bid us welcome,
> We shall come rejoicing, bringing in the sheaves.
>
> Bringing in the sheaves,
> We shall come rejoicing, bringing in the sheaves.

—Knowles Shaw

# Paul's Only Boast Was in the Cross

*But God forbid that I should boast except in the cross of our Lord Jesus Christ, by whom the world has been crucified to me, and I to the world. For in Christ Jesus neither circumcision nor uncircumcision avail anything, but a new creation* (Galatians 6:14, 15).

The Judaizers were pressuring the new Galatian converts to submit to the Jewish circumcision, and were proud to claim their own status as proselytes, but Paul insisted that the only thing that mattered was that Christ died on the cross to justify both Jews and Gentiles. What mattered was that those who believed on Jesus Christ were born again, new creations in Christ.

Paul, who had been an ardent Pharisee, said that his only boast was in the cross of Jesus Christ, since it was the cross on which his sinful old nature had been crucified, and he had received a new identity as a believer in Jesus Christ, his Redeemer.

John Bunyan, in his famous book *Pilgrim's Progress* wrote of Christian's experience at the cross:

"Blest cross, blest sepulchre, blest rather be
The Man that there was put to shame for me."

In the cross of Christ I glory,
Towering o'er the wrecks of time;
All the light of sacred story, gathers round its head sublime.

When the woes of life o'ertake me,
Hopes deceive and fears annoy,
Never shall the cross forsake me,
Lo it glows with peace and joy.

Bane and blessing, pain and pleasure
By the cross are sanctified;
Peace is there that knows no measure,
Joys that through all time abide.

—John Bowring

# Begotten to a Living Hope

*Blessed be the God and Father of our Lord Jesus Christ, who according to His abundant mercy has begotten us again to a living hope through the resurrection of Jesus Christ from the dead, to an inheritance incorruptible and undefiled and that does not fade away, reserved in heaven for you, who are kept by the power of God through faith for salvation ready to be revealed in the last time* (1 Peter 1:3-5).

The apostle Peter wrote to the Jews in the Diaspora of the Asian provinces, to remind them of the rich blessings in store for them in the gospel of Jesus Christ. Among these blessings he mentioned the new birth, the unfading inheritance that was reserved for them in heaven, and the salvation that would be revealed in the last days of the Christian era. They were also to be kept by the power of almighty God. Peter reminded them that the "genuineness of their faith was more precious than gold that perishes" (1 Peter 1:7).

He went on to praise their fidelity: "whom [Jesus Christ] having not seen you love. Though now you do not see Him, yet believing, you rejoice with joy inexpressible and full of glory, receiving the end of your faith—the salvation of your souls (1 Peter 1:8, 9).

More about Jesus would I know,
More of His grace to others show;
More of His saving fullness see,
More of His love who died for me.

More about Jesus let me learn,
More of His holy will discern;
Spirit of God, my teacher be,
Showing the things of Christ to me.

More about Jesus in His Word,
Holding communion with my Lord,
Hearing His voice in every line,
Making each faithful saying mine.

—H. E. Hewitt

# Christ is the Living Stone

*Coming to Him* [Jesus Christ] *as to a living stone, rejected indeed by men, but chosen by God and precious, you also, as living stones, are being built up a spiritual house, a holy priesthood, to offer up spiritual sacrifices acceptable to God through Jesus Christ.... Therefore, to you who believe, He is precious; but to those who are disobedient,... "a stone of stumbling and a rock of offense"* (1 Peter 2:4, 5, 8).

In quoting the prophetic passage from Psalm 118, Peter explained why Christians are offensive to many. Many people, indeed, reverence God, but ignore Jesus Christ. We Christians may be reminders of the One who they would prefer to forget about. But to us who believe, He is precious.

Peter went on to show that God is forming us who believe as spiritual "stones" in a "spiritual house," to the praise of God's glory. Our worship is acceptable to God through Jesus Christ.

To those who despise God's offer of free grace through faith in Jesus Christ, however, He is a "stumbling block and a rock of offense." Jesus warned: "For the Father judges no one, but has committed all judgment to the Son, that all should honor the Son just as they honor the Father. He who does not honor the Son does not honor the Father who sent Him" (John 5:22, 23).

> This is Thy temple-gate, O Lord, the just shall enter there;
> My Savior, I will give Thee thanks,
> O Thou that hearest prayer.

> The stone rejected and despised is now the cornerstone,
> How wondrous are the ways of God,
> Unfathomed and unknown!

> In this the day that Thou hast made, triumphantly we sing;
> Send now prosperity, O Lord,
> O Lord, salvation bring.

—Psalter 318, Psalm 118

# Live Like Pilgrims and Strangers

*Beloved, I beg you as sojourners and pilgrims, abstain from fleshly lusts which war against the soul, having your conduct honorable among the Gentiles, that when they speak against you as evildoers, they may, by your good works which they observe, glorify God in the day of visitation. Therefore submit yourselves to every ordinance of man for the Lord's sake... For this is the will of God, that by doing good you may put to silence the ignorance of foolish men"* (1 Peter 2:11-13a, 15).

One of the major challenges in cross-cultural living is to respect the customs in the community where you are living, and not violate your own. If you violate their customs you are seen as a bad person, but it you feel forced to violate your own, you carry an unhealthy load of guilt. I had never noticed how relevant Peter's counsel is for the cross-cultural gospel worker.

I also noticed that most of my twinges of conscience come from violating some of our cultural norms, rather than from Biblical absolutes. Learn to discern between the two, for your own peace of mind.

> I'm a pilgrim, and I'm a stranger;
> I can tarry, I can tarry but a night;
> Do not detain me, for I am going
> To where the fountains are ever flowing.
>
> There the glory is ever shining;
> O my longing heart, my longing heart is there;
> Here in this country, so dark and dreary,
> I long have wandered forlorn and weary.
>
> There's the city to which I journey;
> My Redeemer, my Redeemer, is its light;
> There is no sinning, nor any sighing,
> Nor any tears there, nor any dying.
>
> I'm a pilgrim, and I'm a stranger;
> I can tarry, I can tarry but a night.

—Mrs. M. S. B. Dana

165

# Called to Suffer

*For to this you were called, because Christ also suffered for us, leaving us an example, that you should follow His steps; "Who committed no sin, nor was deceit found in His mouth", who when He was reviled, did not revile in return; when He suffered, He did not threaten, but committed Himself to Him who judges righteously. Who Himself bore our sins in His own body on the tree, that we, having died to sins, might live for righteousness— "by whose striped you were healed"...* (1 Peter 2:21-24).

The apostle Peter reminded the believers that they ought not to be surprised that suffering became their lot after they believed. After all, Christ suffered for us, bearing our sins in His own body. He urged them to imitate Christ's patience in suffering, by not avenging themselves on their persecutors, nor threatening them.

Jesus taught His disciples: "Blessed are you when they revile and persecute you, and say all kinds of evil against you falsely for My sake. Rejoice and be exceedingly glad, for great is your reward in heaven, for so they persecuted the prophets who were before you" (Matthew 5:11, 12).

I gave my life for thee, my precious blood I shed,
That thou might ransomed be and quickened from the dead.
I gave, I gave my life for thee;
What hast thou given for me?

My Father's house of light, My glory-circled throne
I left for earthly night, for wanderings sad and lone.
I left, I left it all for thee;
What hast thou left for Me?

I suffered much for thee, more than thy tongue can tell,
Of bitterest agony, to rescue thee from hell.
I've borne, I've borne it all for thee;
What hast thou borne for Me?

And I have brought to thee down from my throne above,
Salvation full and free, my pardon and my love...

—Frances R. Havergal

# Love as Brothers

*Finally, all of you be of one mind, having compassion for one another; love as brothers, be tenderhearted, be courteous, not returning evil for evil or reviling for reviling, but on the contrary blessing, knowing that you were called to this, that you may inherit a blessing* (1 Peter 3:8, 9).

After Peter taught the appropriate behaviors between husband and wife, he urged that they should "love as brothers," and treat one another with courtesy. Sometimes it is easier to treat a stranger with courtesy than it is a spouse, but Peter's advice is very pertinent, and could do much to revolutionize marriage relationships.

Note that Peter says that we have been "called to bless others." Let us then strive to be a blessing to all those with whom we come in contact.

> Our Father, Thou in heaven above,
> Who biddest us to dwell in love,
> As brethren of one family.
> And cry for all we need to Thee;
> Teach us to mean the words we say,
> And from the inmost heart to pray.
>
> Thy will be done on earth, O Lord!
> As where in heaven Thou are adored!
> Patience in time of grief bestow,
> Obedience true in weal and woe;
> Our sinful heart and will control
> That thwart Thy will within the soul.
>
> Into temptation lead us not,
> And when the foe doth war and plot,
> Deliverance from all evil give,
> For yet in evil days we live;
> Redeem us from eternal death,
> E'en when we yield our dying breath.
>
> —M. Luther, Tr. Miss C. Winkworth

# Peter Urges Hospitality

*But the end of all things is at hand; therefore be serious and watchful in your prayers. And above all things have fervent love for one another, for "love will cover a multitude of sins" Be hospitable to one another without grumbling. As each one has received a gift, minister it to one another as good stewards of the manifold grace of God* (1 Peter 4:7-10).

Just as in the case of sharing what we have with a needy brother or sister, the opening of our homes to a brother who needs shelter is a very practical way of practicing love to our neighbor.

This is not to say that there is no risk in sharing our shelter and goods with a brother or sister, because we all know of cases where the needy brother or sister took base advantage of someone's hospitality, but theses surely are few in comparison with the blessing and gratitude of the brother or sister who was helped in their hour of need by a hospitable brother or sister.

The unknown writer of the epistle to the Hebrews wrote: "Let brotherly love continue. Do not forget to entertain strangers, for by so doing some have unwittingly entertained angels" (Hebrews 13:1-2).

Mid scenes of confusion, and creature complaints
How sweet to my soul is communion with saints;
To find at the banquet of mercy there's room,
And feel in the presence of Jesus at home!

Sweet home that unites all the children of peace,
And thrice blessed Jesus, whose love cannot cease;
Though oft from Thy presence in sadness I roam,
I long to behold Thee in glory, at home.

I long, dearest Lord, in Thy beauties to shine,
No more as an exile in sorrow to pine.
And in Thy dear image, arise from the tomb,
With glorified millions to praise Thee at home.

—David Denham

# Be Vigilant

*Therefore humble yourselves under the mighty hand of God, that He may exalt you in due time, casting all your care upon Him, for He cares for you. Be sober, be vigilant, because your adversary the devil walks about like a roaring lion, seeking whom he may devour. Resist him, steadfast in the faith, knowing that the same sufferings are experienced by your brotherhood in the world* (1 Peter 5:6-9).

A proud spirit renders us more susceptible to attacks by the devil. Peter urges us to "humble ourselves under God's mighty hand" so that we can repel the devil's attacks. God cares for us, so we need not fear to trust in Him.

Peter, who himself had been trapped by the devil into denying his Master after His arrest, warns the diaspora Christians to be alert to the devil's crafty attacks on God's people. He is a predatory spirit who seeks to destroy God's work in the world. Peter reminds us that all God's people are subject to such demonic attacks, whether in the guise of a good spirit (angel) or as an evil spirit (demon).

An ancient hymn urges us to stand firm against the attacks by the forces of hell:

> Christian, dost thou see them on the holy ground,
> How the hosts of Midian prowl and prowl around?
> Christian, up and smite them, counting gain but loss;
> Smite them, Christ is with thee, soldier of the cross.
>
> Christian, dost thou feel them, how they work within?
> Striving, tempting, luring, goading into sin?
> Christian, up and smite them, never be downcast;
> Gird thee for the battle, watch and pray, and fast.
>
> Christian, dost thou hear them, how they speak thee fair?
> "Always fast and vigil, always watch and prayer."
> Christian, answer boldly, "While I breathe, I pray;"
> Peace shall follow battle, night shall end in day.

—St. Andrew of Crete, 700 AD; Tr. J. M. Neale

# Qualifications of Church Leaders

[Paul wrote:] *For this reason I left you in Crete that you should set in order the things that are lacking, and appoint elders in every city as I commanded you—If a man is blameless, the husband of one wife, having faithful children not accused of dissipation or insubordination. For a bishop must be blameless, as a steward of God, not self-willed, not quick-tempered, not given to wine, not violent, not greedy for money, but hospitable, a lover of what is good, sober-minded, just, holy, self-controlled, holding fast the faithful word as he has been taught, that he may be able, by sound doctrine, both to exhort and convict those who contradict* (Titus 1:6-9).

In specifying what a Christian leader's family should be like, Paul brings to mind the words of Psalm 128 (below). The elder must be able to guide his family in God's ways, if he is expected to guide the Church of Christ in godly paths (see 1 Timothy 3:5).

Although the ability to handle people and funds are important qualities, the candidates for church leadership must be able to demonstrate loving control in their families.

Blest the man that fears Jehovah,
Walking ever in His ways;
By thy toil thou shalt be prospered,
And be happy all thy days.

In thy wife thou shalt have gladness,
She shall fill thy home with good;
Happy in her loving service,
And the joys of motherhood.

Joyful children, sons and daughters,
Shall about thy table meet;
Olive plants, in strength and beauty,
Full of hope and promise sweet.

Lo, on him that fears Jehovah
Shall this blessedness attend,...

—Psalter 360, Psalm 128

# Paul Instructs Young Titus

*For the grace of God that brings salvation has appeared to all men, teaching us that, denying ungodliness and worldly lusts, we should live soberly, righteously, and godly in the present age, looking for the blessed hope and glorious appearing of our great God and Savior Jesus Christ, who gave Himself for us, that He might redeem us from every lawless deed and purify for Himself His own special people, zealous for good works* (Titus 2:11-14).

Paul emphasized that the goal of salvation is to turn sinners into moral images of the Lord Jesus. It is not merely to guarantee them an eternity of bliss, but even in this life, to conform them to be like the Lord Jesus. Therefore we are to live "soberly, righteously, and godly" lives. We ought to be "God's special people, zealous for good works."

We are reminded of Paul's words to the Ephesians: "For we are His workmanship, created in Christ Jesus for good works, which God prepared beforehand that we should walk in them" (Ephesians 2:10).

> When I survey the wondrous cross
> On which the Prince of Glory died,
> My richest gain I count but loss,
> And pour contempt on all my pride.
>
> Forbid it, Lord, that I should boast,
> Save in the death of Christ my God;
> All the vain things that charm me most—
> I sacrifice them to His blood.
>
> See from His head, His hands, His feet,
> Sorrow and love flowed mingled down;
> Did e'er such love and sorrow meet,
> Or thorns compose so rich a crown?
>
> Were the whole realm of nature mine,
> That were a present far too small;
> Love so amazing, so divine,
> Demands my soul, my life, my all.

—Isaac Watts

# A Christian's Duties

*Remind them* [the Cretan Christians] *to be subject to rulers and authorities, to obey, to be ready for every good work, to speak evil of no one, to be peaceable, gentle, showing all humility to all men. For we ourselves were also once foolish, disobedient, deceived, serving various lusts, and pleasures, living in malice and envy, hateful and hating one another.*

*But when the kindness and the love of God our Savior toward man appeared, not by works of righteousness which we have done, but according to His mercy, He saved us, through the washing of regeneration and renewing of the Holy Spirit* (Titus 3:1-5).

Paul reminded Titus that the Cretan Christians should be taught that a godly lifestyle was of primary importance to those who had tasted of the manifold grace of God. Since they had been justified by faith, their lives must now reflect the work of the Holy Spirit in their lives. He wrote: "I want you to affirm constantly, that those who have believed in God should be careful to maintain good works" (Titus 3:8b).

More like the Master I would ever be,
More of His meekness, more humility,
More zeal to labor, more courage to be true,
More consecration for work He bids me do.

More like the Master, is my daily prayer,
More strength to carry the burdens I must bear;
More earnest effort to bring His kingdom in,
More of His Spirit the wanderer to win.

More like the Master I would live and grow,
More of His love to others I would show,
More self-denial, like His in Galilee,
More like the Master I long to ever be.

Take Thou my heart, I would be Thine alone;
Take Thou my heart and make it all Thine own;…

—Charles H. Gabriel

# What to Avoid

*But avoid foolish disputes, genealogies, contentions, and strivings about the law; for they are unprofitable and useless. Reject a divisive man after the first and second admonition knowing that such a person is warped and sinning, being self-condemned.... And let our people also learn to maintain good works, to meet urgent needs, that they may not be unfruitful.* (Titus 3:9-11, 14).

Paul warned against encouraging divisive, quarrelsome persons in the fellowship, since they create confusion and splits in the body. In fact, he recommended that after a first and second warning such a member should be ejected from the fellowship.

He again urges that the members should be taught to maintain good works, as of primary importance. They must be trained to meet the urgent needs of the field workers so that they may succeed in their work of evangelism.

> Speed Thy servants, Savior, speed them,
> Thou art Lord of wind and wave;
> They were bound, but Thou hast freed them,
> Now they go to free the slaves.
> O be with them; 'tis Thine arm alone that saves.
>
> Friends and home and all forsaking,
> Lord, they go at Thy command.
> As their stay Thy promise taking,
> While they traverse sea and land.
> O be with them, lead them safely by the hand.
>
> When no fruit appears to cheer them,
> And they seem to toil in vain,
> Then, in mercy, Lord, draw near them,
> And their sinking hopes sustain;
> Thus supported, let their zeal revive again.
>
> In the midst of opposition,
> Let them trust, O Lord, in Thee;...

—Thomas Kelly

# A Converted Run-Away Slave

*...Though I might be very bold in Christ to command you what is fitting, yet for love's sake I rather appeal to you—being such a one as Paul, the aged, and now also a prisoner of Jesus Christ—I appeal to you for my son Onesimus, whom I have begotten while in my chains, who once was unprofitable to you, but now is profitable to you and to me. I am sending him back. You therefore receive him that is, my own heart, whom I wished to keep with me,...but without your consent I wanted to do nothing, that your good deed might not be by compulsion, as it were, but voluntary* (Philemon 8-14).

The epistle to Philemon is a single-page communication from the imprisoned apostle Paul to his colleague Philemon, reporting the conversion of Philemon's runaway slave Onesimus. Since his conversion this young slave had made himself very useful to the imprisoned evangelist, and he confessed a sincere desire to keep him, but would not do so without the consent of his legal owner, Philemon. The apostle demonstrated the kind of Christian character he promoted to his disciple Titus and in his other epistles. What a pattern for our church leaders!

> I would be true, for there are those who trust me;
> I would pure, for there are those who care.
> I would be strong, for there is much to suffer,
> I would be brave, for there is much to dare.
>
> I would be friend of all—the foe, the friendless
> I would be giving, and forget the gift;
> I would be humble, for I know my weakness;
> I would look up, and laugh, and love, and lift.
>
> I would be prayerful through each busy moment;
> I would be constantly in touch with God.
> I would be tuned to hear His lightest whisper,
> I would have faith to keep the path Christ trod.
>
> —Howard A. Walter

# How to Know God's Will

*My son, if you receive my words, and treasure my commands within you, so that you incline your ear to wisdom, and apply your heart to understanding. Yes, if you cry out for discernment and lift your voice for understanding; if you seek her as silver and search for her as for hidden treasures; then you will understand the fear of the LORD, and find the knowledge of God, for the LORD gives wisdom. From His mouth come knowledge and understanding* (Proverbs 2:1-6); ...

The Sage taught his students the source of all wisdom, which is to be found only in God and His word. He also stressed that God is ready and willing to impart His wisdom to the seeker.

King David sang his praises to the Lord who knew him better than he knew himself. He admitted his inability to hide from God's scrutiny, and begged the Lord to search him and guide him in the right paths.

> O Lord, my inmost heart and thought
> Thy searching eye doth see;
> Where'er I rest, where'er I go,
> My ways are known to Thee.
>
> Each spoken word, each silent thought,
> Thou, Lord, dost understand;
> Before me and behind art Thou,
> Restraining by Thy hand.
>
> From Thee, O Lord, I cannot hide,
> Though darkness cover me;
> The darkness and the light of day
> Are both alike to Thee.
>
> Search me, O God, and know my heart,
> Try me, my thought to know;
> O lead me, if in sin I stray,
> In paths of life to go.

—Psalter 384, Psalm 139

175

# The Sage Counsels

*Let not mercy and truth forsake you; bind them around your neck, write them on the tablet of your heart, and so find favor and high esteem in the sight of God and man.*

*Trust in the LORD with all your heart, and lean not on your own understanding; in all your ways acknowledge Him, and He shall direct your paths.*

*Do not be wise in your own eyes; fear the LORD and depart from evil* (Proverbs 3:3-7).

It is impressive that the Sage joins both mercy and truth as the virtues to which we must cling. Notice that he does not endorse ruthless truth, but urges us to be both truthful and merciful. Think how merciful God has been with you, correcting you with love, truth, and grace!

The Sage reminds us that our comprehension of reality is faulty. God alone sees the situation as it really is, and He offers to guide us in His paths so that we do not err. The Sage also warns us against an arrogance that ignores God's offer of guidance, and presumes to know the entire truth about a crisis situation. How can we—whose experience of life is limited—be sure that our understanding of the facts is accurate? God offers to teach us the way we should go.

Jesus calls me—I must follow, follow Him today;
When His tender voice is pleading how can I delay?

Jesus calls me—I must follow, follow every hour;
Know the blessing of His presence, fullness of His power.

Jesus calls me—I must follow, follow Him alway,
When my Savior goes before me, I can never stray.

Follow, I will follow Thee, my Lord,
Follow every passing day;
My tomorrows are all known to Thee,
Thou wilt lead me all the way.

—Howard L. and Margaret W. Brown

# The Value of Wisdom

*Happy is the man who finds wisdom, and the man who gains understanding, for her proceeds are better than the profits of silver, and her gain than fine gold. She is more precious than rubies, and all the things you may desire cannot compare with her... Her ways are ways of pleasantness, and all her paths are peace* (Proverbs 3:13-15, 17).

The Sage stressed the high value of wisdom, because true wisdom has its source in God. The seeker after wisdom is urged to seek God and His word in order to find it.

The psalmist sought wisdom in God's word and found it to be more valuable than gold and silver. He pleaded with God to give him the wisdom he craved, because he had discerned in God's commandments the wisdom he sought.

> I have followed truth and justice;
> Leave me not in deep distress.
> Be my help and my protection,
> Let the proud no more oppress.
> For Thy word and Thy salvation,
> Lord, my eyes with longing fail;
> Teach Thy statutes to Thy servant;
> Let Thy mercy now prevail.
>
> I am Thine, O give me wisdom,
> Make me know Thy truth, I pray;
> Sinners have despised Thy statutes,
> Now, O Lord, Thy power display.
> Lord, I love Thy good commandments
> And esteem them more than gold;
> All Thy precepts are most righteous;
> Hating sin, to these I hold.

—Psalter 336, Psalm 119

# Wisdom Guarantees Safety

*My son, let them not depart from your eyes—keep sound wisdom and discretion—so they will be life to your soul, and grace to your neck. Then you will walk safely in your way, and your foot will not stumble. When you lie down, you will not be afraid. Yes, you will lie down and your sleep will be sweet. Do not be afraid of a sudden terror, nor of trouble from the wicked when it comes. For the LORD will be your confidence, and will keep your foot from being caught* (Proverbs 3:21-26).

The Sage wrote: "The fear of the LORD is to hate evil. Pride and arrogance and the evil way and the perverse mouth I hate. Counsel is mine, and sound wisdom. I am understanding. I have strength…. I love those who love me, and those who seek me diligently will find me" (Proverbs 8:13, 14, 17).

Here "Wisdom" is the personification of God Himself. David wrote: "How shall a young man cleanse his way? By taking heed according to Your word. With my whole heart I have sought You. Oh, let me not wander from Your commandments! Your word I have hidden in my heart, that I might not sin against You" (Psalm 119:9-11).

Teach me Thy way, O Lord, teach me Thy way!
Thy guiding grace afford; teach me Thy way!
Help me to walk aright, more by faith, less by sight;
Lead me with heavenly light; teach me Thy way!

When doubts and fears arise, teach me Thy way!
When storms o'er spread the skies, teach me Thy way!
Shine through the clouds and rain,
Through sorrow, toil, and pain;
Make Thou my pathway plain; teach me Thy way!

Long as my life shall last, teach me Thy way!
Where'er my lot be cast, teach me Thy way!
Until the race is run, until the journey's done,
Until the crown is won, teach me Thy way!

—B. Mansell Ramsey

# Two Paths

*Do not enter the paths of the wicked, and do not walk in the way of evil. Avoid it, do not travel on it; turn away from it and pass on. For they do not sleep until they have done evil; and their sleep is taken away unless they make someone fall. ...But the path of the just is like the shining sun, that shines ever brighter until the perfect day* (Proverbs 4:14-16, 18).

The Sage warned his students to be careful to avoid evil company and to firmly choose the path of the just, which leads to eternal life and glory. In His Sermon on the Mount, Jesus also stressed the importance of choosing the more obscure, narrow road that leads to life, avoiding the well-traveled wide road that leads to destruction (Matthew 7:13, 14).

Paul wrote: "The foolishness of God is wiser than men, and the weakness of God is stronger than men. For you see your calling, brethren, that not many wise according to the flesh, not many mighty, not many noble, are called, but God has chosen the foolish things off the world to put to shame the wise, and God has chosen the weak things of the world to put to shame the things which are mighty; and the base things of the world and the things which are despised, God has chosen, and the things which are not, to bring to nothing the things that are; ... (1 Corinthians 1:25-28).

When gathering clouds around I view,
And days are dark and friends are few;
On Him I lean who not in vain
Experienced every human pain,
He sees my wants, allays my fears,
And counts and treasures up my tears.

If aught should tempt my soul to stray
From heavenly wisdom's narrow way;
To fly the good I would pursue,
Or do the sin I would not do;
Still, He who felt temptation's power
Shall guard me in that dangerous hour.

—Robert Grant

# What Is Most Important

*Get wisdom! Get understanding! Do not forget, nor turn away from the words of my mouth.... Wisdom is the principal thing; therefore get wisdom, and in all your getting, get understanding. Exalt her, and she will promote you; she will bring you honor when you embrace her. She will place on your head an ornament of grace; a crown of glory she will deliver to you* (Proverbs 4:5, 7-9).

The Sage continued his warning: "Keep your heart with all diligence, for out of it spring the issues of life. Put away from you a deceitful mouth, and put perverse lips far from you... Do not turn to the right or to the left; remove your foot from evil" (Proverbs 4:23, 24, 27).

Later the Sage reveals the identity of wisdom and knowledge: "The fear of the LORD is the beginning of wisdom, and the knowledge of the Holy One is understanding. For by me your days will be multiplied, and years of life will be added to you" (Proverbs 9:10, 11).

The largest chapter in the Bible (Psalm 119) is mostly devoted to the psalmist's plea for God's wisdom, promoting the writer's love of the law (scriptures).

> Teach me, O Lord, Thy way of truth,
> And from it I will not depart;
> That I may steadfastly obey,
> Give me an understanding heart.
>
> In Thy commandments make me walk,
> For in Thy law my joy shall be;
> Give me a heart that loves Thy will,
> From discontent and envy free.
>
> Turn Thou my eyes from vanity,
> And cause me in Thy ways to tread;
> O let Thy servant prove Thy word
> And thus to godly fear be lead.

—Psalter 325, Psalm 119

# Jesus Prays for You

[Jesus prayed:] *I pray for them* [the disciples]. *I do not pray for the world, but for those whom you have given Me, for they are Yours.... I do not pray that You should take them out of the world, but that You should keep them from the evil one.... I do not pray for these alone, but also for those who will believe on Me through their word* (John 17:9, 15).

*Therefore He* [Jesus] *is also able to save to the uttermost those who come to God by Him, since He always lives to make intercession for them* (Hebrews 7:25).

Did you know that the Lord Jesus prayed for you just before He went to the cross (see John 17:9, 15, above)? He prayed first for His disciples, then He extended the prayer to include all those who would eventually believe on Him through their witness, which we have recorded in our Bibles.

As if that were not enough, the author to the Hebrews says that even today "He ever lives to make intercession for those who come to God by Him."

What a gracious, faithful Savior!

> Arise, my soul, arise! Shake off thy guilty fears;
> The bleeding Sacrifice on thy behalf appears;
> Before the throne my Surety stands,
> My name is written on His hands.
>
> He ever lives above for me to intercede;
> His all-redeeming love, His precious blood to plead.
> His blood atoned for all our race,
> And sprinkles now the throne of grace.
>
> Five bleeding wounds He bears, received on Calvary;
> They pour effectual prayers, they strongly plead for me;
> "Forgive him, O forgive," they cry,
> "Nor let the ransomed sinner die!"

—Charles Wesley

# Jesus' Name Is "Wonderful"

*For unto us a Child is born, unto us a Son is given; and the government shall be upon His shoulder, and His name will be called "Wonderful, Counselor, Mighty God, Everlasting Father, Prince of Peace. Of the increase of His government and peace there will be no end, upon the throne of David and over His kingdom, to order it and establish it with judgment and justice, from that time forward, even forever...* (Isaiah 9:6-7).

Some time in the 1970s Harold and I translated some worship songs into the Maxakali language. I recall hearing an old Indian woman say to her companion, "Jesus! What a beautiful name!"

All she knew was the name, yet she sensed the beauty and majesty of it. I was deeply moved. Our hymnody resounds with praises to His wonderful name. All eternity will echo with His praises.

Paul wrote: "[He] made Himself of no reputation, taking on Himself the form of a bondservant... He humbled Himself and became obedient to the point of death, even the death of the cross. Therefore God also has highly exalted Him and given Him the name which is above every name, that at the name of Jesus every knee should bow. ... (Philippians 2:7a, 8b, 9, 10a).

> Join all the glorious names of wisdom, love, and power,
> That ever mortals knew, that angels ever bore;
> All are too mean to speak His worth,
> To mean to set my Savior forth.

> I love my Shepherd's voice, His watchful eye shall keep
> My wandering soul among the thousands of His sheep;
> He feeds His flock, He calls their names,
> His bosom bears the tender lambs.

> My Savior and my Lord, my Conqueror and my King,
> Thy scepter and Thy sword, Thy reigning grace I sing;
> Thine is the power; behold I sit
> In willing bonds beneath Thy feet.

—Isaac Watts

# God Swears His Offer is Sincere

*"As I live," says the LORD God, "I have no pleasure in the death of the wicked, but that the wicked turn from his ways and live. Turn, turn, from your evil ways! For why should you die, O house of Israel! ...When I say to the wicked, "You shall surely die, if he turns from his sin and does what is lawful and right,... if he ... walks in the statutes of life without committing iniquity, he shall surely live, he shall not die. None of his sins which he has committed shall be remembered against him...* (Ezekiel 33:14b, 15b, 16).

Ezekiel was called to be a prophet to the exiled citizens of Judah during this dark period. God had punished the wayward Israelites for their neglect of His laws and their rampant idolatry by allowing the Babylonians to conquer Judah and take all its prominent citizens as slaves to neighboring countries. Yet God remembered His promise to the patriarchs, and offered them pardon if they would abandon their sinful practices and return to the Lord.

Friends, God has not changed. He has no pleasure in seeing that the wicked get what they deserve. He delights in mercy, and offered to forgive them if they repented of their unfaithfulness to Him. He offers the same to you.

> Marvelous grace of our loving Lord,
> Grace that exceeds our sin and our guilt!
> Yonder on Calvary's mount outpoured—
> There where the blood of the Lamb was spilt.
>
> Sin and despair like the sea-waves cold,
> Threaten the soul with infinite loss;
> Grace that is greater, yes grace untold,
> Points to the refuge, the mighty cross.
>
> Dark is the stain that we cannot hide,
> What can avail to wash it away?
> Look! There is flowing a crimson tide—
> Whiter than snow you may be today.

—Julia H. Johnston

# God Comforts His People

*Sing, O heavens! Be joyful, O earth! And break out in singing, O mountains! For the LORD has comforted His people, and will have mercy on His afflicted.*

*But Zion said, "The LORD has forsaken me, and my LORD has forgotten me."*

*Can a woman forget her nursing child, and not have compassion on the son of her womb? Surely they may forget, yet I will not forget you. See, I have inscribed you on the palms of My hands; your walls are continually before Me* (Isaiah 49:13-16).

Surely these verses are among the most comforting in all of scripture. However distant we may be from the standard the Lord has set for his human creatures, He is faithful to His promises. He will not forget us.

Who else can we turn to, in our need? We are indelibly inscribed on His hands; those hands that were pierced on the cross for our sins, and are now extended to us in an offer of grace.

> The Lord upholds the faltering feet,
> And makes the weak securely stand;
> The burdened ones, bowed down with grief
> Are helped by His most gracious hand.
> The eyes of all upon Thee wait,
> By Thee their wants are all supplied;
> Thy open hand is bountiful,
> And every soul is satisfied.

> The Lord is just in all His ways,
> In all His works the Lord is kind;
> And all that call on Him in truth
> In Him a present helper find.
> He will fulfill the heart's desire
> Of those that fear Him and obey,
> Their cry the Lord will surely hear,
> And He will answer when they pray.

—Psalter 398, Psalm 145

# God Promises a Bright Future

*And on this mountain the LORD will make for all people a feast of choice pieces, a feast of wines on the lees, of well-refined wines on the lees. And He will destroy on this mountain the surface of the covering cast over all people, and the veil that is spread over the nations. He will swallow up death forever. And the Lord GOD will wipe away tears from all faces. The rebuke of His people He will take away from the earth; for the LORD has spoken* (Isaiah 25:6-8).

In this paragraph God promises to prepare a feast to which "all people" will be invited. He further promises to destroy the veil that had been spread over the nations. He does not specify what this "veil" is, but it may be death itself, which He will abolish forever.

He also promises to "wipe away tears from all faces," which prophecy is repeated in Revelation: "And God will wipe away every tear from their eyes. There shall be no more death, nor sorrow, nor crying. There shall be no more pain, for the former things have passed away. And He that sat on the throne said 'Behold, I make all things new'" (Revelation 21:4, 5a).

On Jordan's stormy banks I stand
And cast a wishful eye,
To Canaan's fair and happy land
Where my possessions lie.

All o'er those wide-extended plains
Shines one eternal day,
Where God the Son forever reigns
And scatters night away.

No chilling winds nor poisonous breath
Can reach that healthful shore;
Sickness and sorrow, pain and death
Are felt and feared no more.

—Samuel Stennett

# God's Lifelong Care

[God said,] *Listen to Me, O house of Jacob, and all the remnant of the house of Israel, who have been upheld by Me from birth, who have been carried from the womb: Even to your old age, I am He, and even to gray hairs I will carry you! I have made, and I will bear; even I will carry, and will deliver you.*

*To whom will you liken Me, and make Me equal, and compare Me, that we should be alike?* (Isaiah 46:3-5).

Through the prophet Isaiah, God repeated His pledge to be the God of His people forever. Israel and Judah had forsaken the laws of their God and had thrown themselves fully into the worship of the false gods of the neighboring pagan countries. They had also abandoned the civil laws God had instituted for the welfare of the whole society, and were enriching themselves at the expense of the underprivileged, such as the widows, orphans, and aliens. For many years God had sent prophets to warn them of the consequences of their disloyalty, but they had not been heeded.

Finally, God reminded them of His faithfulness and asked whether they had found any heathen gods who offered them the same protection. Since these gods had no real existence, they could not protect anyone,

I take Thy promise, Lord, in all its length,
And breadth, and fullness, as my daily strength;
Into life's future, fearless I may gaze,
For, Jesus, Thou art with me all the days.

There may be days of darkness and distress,
When sin has power to tempt, and care to press,
Yet, in the darkest day I will not fear,
For, mid the shadows, Thou wilt still be near.

Days there may be of joy, and deep delight,
When earth seems fairest, and her skies most bright;
Then draw me closer to Thee, lest I rest
Elsewhere, my Savior, than upon Thy breast.

—H. L. R. Deck

# God's Open Invitation

[God said:] *Look to Me, and be saved, all you ends of the earth. For I am God, and there is no other. I have sworn by Myself; the word has gone out of My mouth in righteousness, and shall not return, that to Me every knee shall bow, every tongue shall take an oath* (Isaiah 45:22, 23).

[Paul wrote:] *God also has highly exalted Him [Jesus] and given Him the name which is above every name, that at the name of Jesus every knee should bow, of those in heaven, and of those on earth, and of those under the earth; and that every tongue should confess that Jesus Christ is Lord, to the glory of God the Father* (Philippians 2:9-11).

Dear friends, God is glorified when Jesus Christ is praised. He has determined that all people will bow to His Son in adoration and acknowledge His authority over the universe.

> Look, ye saints, the sight is glorious,
> See the "Man of Sorrows" now;
> From the fight returned victorious,
> Every knee to Him shall bow!
> Crown Him! crown Him!
> Crowns become the Victor's brow.
>
> Sinners in derision crowned Him,
> Mocking thus the Savior's claim;
> Saints and angels crowd around Him,
> Own His title, praise His name;
> Crown Him! crown Him!
> Spread abroad the Victor's fame.
>
> Hark, the burst of acclamation!
> Hark, those loud triumphant chords!
> Jesus takes the highest station,
> Oh, what joy the sight affords!
> Crown Him! Crown Him,
> "King of kings, and Lord of lords!"

—Thomas Kelly

# Christ Will also Redeem the Gentiles

*Indeed He* [God] *says, "It is too small a thing that You should be My Servant to raise up the tribes of Jacob, and to restore the preserved ones of Israel. I will also give You as a light to the Gentiles, that You should be My salvation to the ends of the earth"* (Isaiah 49:6).

Throughout the Old Testament we see hints that God meant to extend His salvation to the entire Gentile world. Here in His message to Isaiah He was very specific that His grace would the extended to all nations.

In His message of comfort to the exiled nations of Israel and Judah, God made no secret of His plans to extend His salvation to the remotest parts of the earth. We Europeans, as well as the Israelites, have been close to despising certain people groups and have been very slow to extend the gospel of free grace to them. But as early as Abraham's day, God stated that His goal was to bless all people of the earth through Abraham's descendant.

My God, I will extol Thee and ever bless Thy Name;
Each day will I give thanks to Thee
And all Thy praise proclaim.
Great is the Lord and mighty, and highly to be praised;
His greatness is unsearchable,
Above our knowledge raised.

The Lord is very gracious and most compassionate,
His anger is most slow to rise, His mercy is most great.
On all His helpless creatures His tender mercies rest,
By all His works He shall be praised,
By all His saints be blest.

The glory of His kingdom proclaimed abroad shall be,
That all may know His mighty deeds and glorious majesty.
His kingdom is eternal, His throne shall stand secure,
And His dominion without end through ages shall endure.

—Psalter 399, Psalm 145

# God Gives Light to the Nations

*Thus says God the LORD, who created the heavens and stretched them out, who spread forth the earth and that which comes from it, who gives breath to the people on it, and spirit to those who walk on it. "I, the LORD, have called You in righteousness and will hold Your hand. I will keep You and give You as a covenant to the people, as a light to the Gentiles.... I am the LORD, that is My name, and My glory I will not give to another, nor My praise to carved images* (Isaiah 42:5-6, 8).

In this prophecy, Isaiah foretold the spread of the gospel to the Gentile world, with the sending of the good news to those who had never heard. Since God would spread His glory to the Gentiles as well as the Jews, Jesus commanded that His emissaries should "go into all the world and preach the gospel to every creature. He who believes and is baptized will be saved; but he who does not believe will be condemned.... And they went and preached everywhere,..." (Mark 16:15, 16, 20a).

Dear friend, "God is not willing that any should perish, but that all should come to repentance" (2 Peter 3:9b). He is worthy of the praise of all of His creatures.

> Ancient of Days, who sittest throned in glory,
> To Thee all knees are bent, all voices pray;
> Thy love hast blest the wide world's wondrous story
> With light and life since Eden's dawning day.
>
> O Holy Father, who hast led Thy children
> In all the ages, with the fire and cloud,
> Through seas dry-shod, through weary wastes bewildering,
> To Thee, in reverent love, our hearts are bowed.
>
> O Triune God, with heart and voice adoring,
> Praise we the goodness that doth crown our days;
> Pray we that Thou wilt hear us, still imploring
> Thy love and favor, kept to us always.

—William C. Doane

# God Guarantees His Salvation

[God said,] *Lift up your eyes to the heavens, and look on the earth beneath, for the heavens will vanish away like smoke. The earth will grow old like a garment, and those who dwell in it will die in like manner, but My salvation will be forever, and My righteousness will not be abolished.... For the moth will eat them* [their reproaches] *up like a garment, and the worm will eat them like wool, but My righteousness will be forever, and My salvation from generation to generation* (Isaiah 51:6, 8).

The prayer in Psalm 102 is attributed to "the afflicted," who is not named, but the introduction says that "he was overwhelmed, and poured out his complaint to the Lord."

In my lifetime I have undergone many changes, but God reassured the people of Isaiah's day that He will never change, and that His salvation is guaranteed forever. We can depend on His word. He told the ungrateful Israelites who returned from exile: "I am the Lord, I do not change; therefore you are not consumed, O sons of Jacob" (Malachi 3:6).

Thou, O Lord, art God alone,
Everlasting is Thy throne;
Through the ages men shall sing
Praise to heaven's eternal King.

Thou enthroned above the skies
Wilt for Zion's help arise;
Let Thy grace to her appear,
For the promised time is near.

This all ages shall record
For the glory of the Lord.
Thou dost hear the humble prayer
For the helpless in Thy care.

Thou eternal art, and great,
Heaven and earth Thou didst create;
Heaven and earth shall pass away,
Changeless Thou shalt live for aye.

—Psalter 275, Psalm 102

190

# The Lord is Your Keeper

*The LORD is your keeper; the LORD is your shade at your right hand. The sun shall not strike you by day, nor the moon by night. The LORD will preserve you from all evil; He shall preserve your soul. The LORD shall preserve your going out and your coming in from this time forth, and even forevermore* (Psalm 121:5-8).

This is one of the "psalms of ascents" which were sung by men who were traveling to the temple for one of the obligatory feasts. It is a comforting psalm for the elderly, who suffer from risks of crippling falls. Falls from which some elderly people never fully recover.

It is also a comforting psalm for those who suffer from insomnia. Since it promises that "He who keeps you will not slumber. Behold, He who keeps Israel will neither slumber nor sleep" (verses 3b and 4). We are never alone during the long, sleepless nights, but our Keeper watches over us.

For the traveler it is also a source of comfort, because it affirms that 'the LORD shall preserve your going out and your coming in from this time forth and forevermore" (verse 8).

David sang: "Surely goodness and mercy shall follow me all the days of my life, and I shall dwell in the house of the LORD forever" (Psalm 23:6).

To the hills I lift my eyes; whence shall help for me arise?
From the Lord shall come my aid,
Who the heaven and earth has made.
He will guide through dangers all, will not suffer thee to fall;
He who safe His people keeps,
Slumbers not, and never sleeps.

Thy protector is the Lord; shade for thee He will afford;
Neither sun nor moon shall smite,
God shall guard by day and night.
He will ever keep thy soul; what would harm He will control.
In the home and by the way,
He will keep thee day by day.

—Psalter 345, Psalm 121

191

# Teach Me, Lord

*I remember the days of old; I meditate on all Your works. I muse on the work of Your hands. I spread out my hands to You; my soul longs for You like a thirsty land.... Cause me to hear Your lovingkindness in the morning, for in You do I trust. Cause me to know the way in which I should walk, for I lift up my soul to You.... Teach me to do Your will, for You are my God. Your Spirit is good. Lead me in the land of uprightness* (Psalm 143:5, 6, 8, 10).

David, the "man after God's own heart," owned that he needed God's teaching in order to live up to God's requirements. He reminded God of all His blessings in the past, and longed to feel God's loving presence in his present life, teaching him how to live.

The Lord Jesus told his disciples on the night He was betrayed, that He would send the Holy Spirit to guide them in their spiritual journey: "The Helper, the Holy Spirit, whom the Father will send in My name, He will teach you all things, and bring to your remembrance all the things that I said to you" (John 14:26). And on the day of His ascension, He reminded them to "tarry in the city of Jerusalem until you are endued with power from on high" (Luke 24:49).

Oh, teach me what it meaneth—Thy love beyond compare;
The love that reacheth deeper than depths of self-despair!
Yes, teach me, till there gloweth in this cold heart of mine
Some feeble, pale reflection of that pure love of Thine.

Oh teach me what it meaneth, for I am full of sin;
And grace alone can reach me, and love alone can win.
Oh, teach me, for I need Thee—I have no hope beside—
The chief of all the sinners for whom the Savior died!

O Infinite Redeemer! I bring no other plea,
Because Thou dost invite me, I cast myself on Thee.
Because Thou dost accept me, I love and I adore;
Because Thy love constraineth, I'll praise Thee evermore!

—Lucy A. Bennett

# Love that Passes Knowledge

*For this reason I bow my knees to the Father of our Lord
Jesus Christ... that He would grant you according to the riches of
His glory to be strengthened with might in the inner man, that
Christ may dwell in your hearts through faith, that you being
rooted and grounded in love, may be able to comprehend with all
the saints what is the width and length and depth and height—to
know the love of Christ which passes knowledge, that you may be
filled with all the fullness of God* (Ephesians 3:14, 16-19).

With these amazing words the apostle Paul prayed that God
would grant the Ephesian Christians (and us) to experience the
love of Christ, which "passes knowledge."

Dear friend, when Christ "dwells in our hearts through faith,"
we may begin to understand His immense love for us. Although
we cannot know all its dimensions in this life, yet we may
experience a beginning of "all the fullness of God." David sang,
"How precious is your loving kindness, O God! Therefore the
children of men put their trust under the shadow of Your wings"
(Psalm 35:7).

> Although I cannot sing or tell or know
> The fullness of Thy love while here below,
> My empty vessel I may freely bring
> O Thou, who are of love the living spring:
> My vessel fill.
>
> I am an empty vessel, not one thought
> Or look of love I ever to Thee brought,
> Yet I may come and come again to Thee
> With this, the empty sinner's only plea:
> Thou lovest me.
>
> Oh, fill me, Jesus, Savior, with Thy love;
> Lead, lead me to the living fount above;
> Thither may I in simple faith draw nigh,
> And never to another fountain fly
> But unto Thee.

—Mary Shekleton